"Some books are written; others are borne from the depths of lived experience. *Silent Losses* weaves an achingly personal family journey with profound truths about a subject too often cloaked in silence. This is not merely a memoir of loss; it is a testament to transformation.

"Through this story, the author reminds us that even in the depths of despair, there is the possibility of turning pain into purpose, of finding meaning amid the broken pieces of a family's history. It is not just a recounting of events; it is an invitation to reflect, to feel, and to act. It asks us to look beyond the systems we rely upon and to consider their human impact. It compels us to question the silences we accept in our own families and the ways we confront—or avoid—our deepest wounds.

"*Silent Losses* is a deeply moving journey of redemption and hope. The author's courage to share this journey is a gift to us all—a reminder that the act of giving voice can illuminate paths for others and begin to mend even the heaviest of hearts."

~ John J. Beranek, owner of Intersections Consulting

"A heartwarming story of a sister's unconditional love and a saddening reminder of the heartbreak that children with disabilities and their families faced not that long ago. This book is a powerful reminder, especially now, that we must never stop advocating for the rights of those with disabilities so that no family faces this reality again."

~ Amy Jo Yost, education specialist, Northwest Area Cooperative

"I was tearful throughout this memoir, a deeply heartfelt and painfully honest tribute to the author's little sister, whose right to reach her full potential was dishonored. Not only does the reader develop increased compassion for fellow humans with disabilities, but Barb Avery-Sterud reveals the 'family injury' when parents and siblings endure separation due to institutionalization. This book is a treasure trove for laypersons and professionals wishing to understand further the stark realities of long-term placement away from one's family. Barb's life experience, extensive education, life-long advocacy, and sisterly love provide the reader with thought-provoking commentary about proper education for vulnerable students. *Silent Losses* is a well-spring of personal memories that enlightens the reader about doing what's right … for one's entire family."

~ Sue Williams, licensed marriage and family therapist

"A heartfelt memoir of love, resilience, and growth, *Silent Losses: The Trauma of Institutionalizing Children* delivers a poignant and deeply personal account of life with a younger sister who had cerebral palsy. This memoir is far more than a medical narrative—it is a love letter to the sibling bond, a testament to the resilience of the human spirit, and a reflection on how differences damage, shape, and ultimately enrich family dynamics.
"With a voice that is both tender and candid, Barb details a shared childhood filled with moments of laughter, frustration, and unconditional love."

~ Dr. C.J. Carmody

"Not only is the narrative compelling, but it also shows the lasting impacts of prior approaches to education and care of individuals with disabilities. Each reader will find particular threads that resonate and hopefully lead to positive change for families, children, siblings, therapists, teachers, and other practitioners."

~ Dr. Marje Kaiser, superintendent for the South Dakota School for the Blind and Visually Impaired, 1960-2020; South Dakota School for the Deaf, 2020

"Well, once again, you have amazed me! Your book was fantastic and portrayed so much of what most of us who have family members with a disability must have encountered sometime in our lives. This was so beautifully captured through humor, honest raw feelings, education, and genuine love! Great job. I am so super proud of you and can't wait for it to be published. I want my mom to read this, too, because she had a sister that had a traumatic brain injury and was sent away, and I think it will resonate loudly with her as well."

~ Lisa Fowler, American Sign Language interpreter

"This book is so moving and heart-wrenching. As an empath, you took in everyone's feelings and reactions. Thank you for telling Pam's story, which would never have been told without you."

~ Susan Beyenhof, MSW

"Barb's memoir bravely shares the impact a child with special needs has on a family. When I worked with Barb in the early '70s, I was unaware she had a sister with special needs who resided at Custer State Hospital, our state institution that served the most severely impaired. I did not know the hurt within Barb, but I can say I did see Barb as one of the most caring, sensitive caregivers I have known in my many years in the field of special education. The children she cared for at what was then called Redfield State Hospital were blessed to have her relate to them as not just another staff member but perhaps as a 'sister.' *Silent Losses* is truly important in many ways, as it documents the realities families face and gives us a glimpse back to the '60s when, as a society, we missed the mark for many children with disabilities and their families. Barb's journey and insights as a sister of someone with a disability to a special educator with an EdD is indeed unique. I am grateful she chose to share her invaluable perspectives with us."

~ Paula Platz, retired assistant professor of special education, Dakota Wesleyan University

SILENT
LOSSES

SILENT LOSSES

THE TRAUMA OF

INSTITUTIONALIZING

CHILDREN

BARBARA AVERY-STERUD, EdD

AWAKEN  VILLAGE
—— PRESS ——

This is a work of nonfiction. The names and identifying characteristics of some persons described in this book have been changed. All events described herein are all true from the author's memory and perspective.

The content of this book is for general instruction only. Each person's physical, emotional, and spiritual condition is unique.

Editing by: Grace Watson
Cover and interior design by: Andrea Gibb
Author photo by: Maddie Peschong

To contact the author or for permission requests, email:
baveryst@gmail.com

ISBN 978-1-957408-18-7 (paperback)
ISBN 978-1-957408-19-4 (ebook)

Library of Congress Control Number: 2024924848

Published by Awaken Village Press
Sioux Falls, South Dakota, U.S.A.
www.awakenvillage.com

For Pamela Sue Avery
I wouldn't change you for
the world, but I would
change the world for you.

There is no greater agony than bearing an untold story inside you.

~ *Maya Angelou*

I often passed the Door of Dreams
  But never stepped inside,
Though sometimes, with surprise, I saw
  The door was open wide.

I might have gone forever by,
  As I had done before,
But one day, when I passed, I saw
  You standing in the door.

- Jessie B. Rittenhouse

PREFACE

W hen I was in college, taking courses that would prepare me to teach elementary and special education, I came across a textbook reference to *A Difference in the Family*, a book by Helen Featherstone that was published in 1981. Featherstone wrote with insight about the experiences of being a "normal" child in a family of a child with a disability, capturing the loneliness and isolation that commonly affects non-handicapped siblings:

> A child's disability can isolate brothers and sisters in several ways. Inside the home, the disability sometimes inhibits communication. A mild or ambiguous handicap may go unlabeled or even unacknowledged. The sense that an important subject is taboo—and the anger that comes with such a realization—cuts children off from their parents, creating embarrassment and reservation. Even in households where candor reigns, children hesitate to reveal ugly feelings. The able-bodied children in very small families some-

times endure a particularly poignant sort of loneliness, a longing for a "real" brother or sister with whom they might share more, one who could reflect their own feelings and experiences.

Featherstone's words resonated with me. As the sister of a child with a disability, I can easily relate to these feelings of isolation and loneliness. Although I was not aware of the impact of these feelings related to inhibited communication at the time, it has become glaringly obvious to me by now.

My sister, Pamela Sue, was born with cerebral palsy and cognitive disabilities in 1960. At that time, the professional advice given to families with disabled children was to institutionalize them as soon as possible, giving everyone permission to move forward and not look back. This plan was presented to families with the idea that moving them to an institution was for the sake of the other children. By that logic, moving my sister somewhere else would supposedly provide opportunities for me and my brothers to experience a "normal family." However, growing up without our sister, knowing she left because that's what was apparently best for us, was anything but normal—for any of us.

Recently, I read an *Atlantic* article entitled "The Ones We Sent Away" by Jennifer Senior. In an interview that followed with Tonya Mosley, recorded on August 10, 2023, Mosley acknowledged that Senior's writing must have been like opening "the closed door of the psyche." In response, Senior explained that the experience was like "nailing things under the floorboard ... but every once in a while you'll hear this thing scratching underneath ...."

This struck me, as I had lived much of my life with my sister in the background but always there. During the times she was more present in my mind, I heard that scratching under the floorboard.

The heartache and loneliness I felt after my sister went to an institution never dissipated. Pam's presence—and absence—gave me gifts of empathy, compassion, and a rich and rewarding career that allowed me to help others through their pain. Despite the challenges of saying goodbye to her when she was just six years old and I was eight, I knew early on that I wanted to help children with disabilities and their families. Pamela gave me the knowledge that the needs of families had to be honored and their voices heard.

I have had the privilege of being a teacher in a variety of settings and have always believed that building relationships with families is of the utmost importance. During my time in this role, I have worked with children and adults in a state hospital setting, young children with physical and cognitive disabilities in a specialized public school program, adolescents adjudicated by the court to complete a correctional program stay, and children aged six to thirteen at a residential treatment program—many with emotional and behavioral difficulties and some placed there by the Department of Social Services due to difficulties within their family structure or while awaiting court decisions about returning to their families. I have also worked as a special education supervisor in a public school setting, with supervision responsibilities for related services such as occupational or physical therapy, speech and language therapy, as well as those provided by teachers of the deaf and teachers of the blind and visually impaired.

In terms of understanding and coming to terms with a child's disability and what it means for the family, I find that I linger in this space today. Recognizing behavior patterns within my family and coming to terms with my own communication and patterned responses have provided insight in ways I couldn't have imagined.

In every position I have held and every program I have played a part in developing, whether working with children or their parents, I have been blessed to be one person who is able to personally relate to what their experience has been, even when those experiences are uniquely different from my own. I am beyond proud of the changes I have been able to take part in making, including my ability to present information and ask questions that spark students' curiosities and challenge them to perhaps look at the subject matter before them in a different way.

I experienced this when I was taking classes, knowing that a few years of learning experience before entering their classrooms would give me something on which to hang the new information I was absorbing. Then, too, I believe my life experience gave me an unexpected advantage in learning. What these programs emphasized in common were (1) intervention into families through another agency's control, (2) families not always being regarded as key players in decision-making, and (3) parents of children with disabilities being viewed as unable to adequately care for them.

These viewpoints were present in my own life experience, and I wasn't sure if I agreed with the consensus.

The current political climate has brought me back to my focus on this topic and my goal of writing my book about Pamela. In my search for information, I was excited to find a dissertation written by a woman named Madeline Burghardt. It included the historical background of institutionalization in Canada as well as interviews with survivors, their parents, and their siblings. She also interviewed former staff and key informants to tell their stories.

Fascinated, I read the whole thing, stopping here and there to dry a few tears. I was so grateful to find this resource, to hear the stories she wrote about the families. Very often, I felt as if she was describing my own.

After more searching, I found her contact information, and one rainy afternoon, I wrote an email to Madeline, introducing myself and letting her know how meaningful her dissertation had been to me, that it was like reading my own history. Thinking I would never hear from her, I felt good at least to have acknowledged her work.

By the end of the afternoon, I had received a response from her along with an invitation to talk with her more about her journey. I was surprised by how this connection had fallen into place, and I knew my sister and guardian angels meant for me to find her without really searching. We set up time to talk later in the week. When we did, Madeline elaborated on a number of matters that were of great import to us both. We discussed siblings' stories of debilitating effects on their families and mothers who had been described as unable to meet the needs of their other children and then never truly recovered from sending their child away. Many mothers who gave birth to children with disabilities never came home from the hospital with them, as they were sent to institutions as infants, never even given the chance to see if a comfortable, successful life could be found at home with their families. So many of my own experiences were validated in this wonderful conversation.

As we were wrapping up, I thought about all I wanted to say in this book, and Pamela Sue had a few things to add. She has been by my side since its very beginning, and her spirit has guided me many times—listening and finding and showing me things that I was looking for to help me tell her story.

There were certain items I knew I had and wanted to refer

to in my writing process but hadn't been able to find. I reorganized my office several times, certain I would run across them—to no avail. One day, I woke up early and looked for Pam's funeral brochure because the dates I had in my head just didn't seem right. I was barely awake when I went back into my office to look once again at the shelves I had already searched.

I don't have the words to explain, but Pam was there, telling me that the things I was looking for were in the storage box with the pink lid. I located the box, opened it, and found the items I had been searching for—the bulletin from her funeral, family photos, a poem our brother had written. She was with me, keeping me on track when I was frustrated about my inability to keep everything organized.

Pamela Sue's encouragement has reinforced why it is so important for me to tell her story—our story. I want readers to understand that techniques and curricula for students with disabilities change for the better as we become more open to learning new things.

This book has been a vision of mine for many years—a vision I believe Pamela Sue shares with me. She has guided my journey to create this book, remaining by my side and encouraging me to keep writing even during the hardest points in the process. My experience of growing up without her yet always feeling her presence has supported me in the ways that matter most.

Thinking back to my college days and the book by Helen Featherstone that meant so much to me, I want to leave my reader with this: "All the members of a family are immensely vulnerable to one another. The pain of one child's disability reshapes every life in unexpected ways. Nonetheless, individuals endure. Each learns ways to live with pain, to alter and even banish much of it. Each experiments with different ways of

being. Each makes a life—often a good one—out of a difference in the family."

With love, I dedicate this to Pamela Sue Avery for all that she
went through during her time on Earth.

Please don't let your hearts break thinking of all that I missed.

I know how you are missing me today,

Wondering what I would think and feel on a day like today.

Please don't think you can't be happy because I'm gone.

I feel joy, and I like to celebrate when there are happy times, or when

One of my favorite staff caring for me is laughing like she does.

My situation does not change. Know that you can say my name out loud.

Know that I am there with you,

At all of your celebrations.

- Barb Avery-Sterud

FAMILY ARCHIVES

It was Thanksgiving of 1985. *How was that possible?* I pondered this as I bundled up my children—Travis, who was three years old, and Amber, who was six years old. The temperature outside was six degrees below zero on that day, so they needed extra bundling. We didn't live far from my parents' home in Redfield, South Dakota, only a few blocks away. It was just the three of us, as I was recently divorced from my children's father, trying to navigate the changes in our little family, and I helped them into their winter gear with talk about the Thanksgiving Day Parade on television—we didn't want to be late for that! I also didn't want to be too late to help my mother with the dinner, knowing she would have gotten up at about four in the morning to get the turkey prepared and in the oven. So we were soon in the car and excited to get to Grandma's.

My parents' home was always warm and welcoming to all who entered, and wonderful smells greeted us as we walked in through the back porch. Already, there were pies and other things balancing on top of the chest freezer. Once unbundled, the three of us entered the kitchen, and both of my parents came over to greet us. Grandpa quickly went back to the living room where the parade was playing on the television, the children following.

My younger brother, Martin, home from college at USD, joined us a little later. We had always been close but became even more so once I was a young mother, he being so supportive to me and the little ones when the divorce was imminent. Uncle Martin was our hero in many ways. We had missed him the first months of his freshman year, and it was so good to see him.

The guests we were still waiting for were my older brother, Wayne, and his daughter, Robin. Folks around here measured things in clock time rather than miles, and they lived about two hours from Redfield, in Brookings. When they arrived, sometime between the start of the parade and dinner getting on the table, Amber and Travis were in the toy room, which was also the sewing room and my former bedroom. I had painted it a lovely shade of purple to go with the purple shag carpet, now looking a bit worse for wear.

Robin, soon to be twelve, loved seeing my kiddos, and we didn't see her and her dad very often. She quickly joined them in the room to play with the toys and coloring books, complete with an old ice cream bucket filled with crayons, many of them broken and down to the nib. My mother was very frugal, and new crayons were just as rare during my kids' childhoods as they had been when I was their age.

Once we all came together around the table, Martin and Wayne talked about college life and how different their experiences were. When Wayne entered college, he was married and started second semester with a new baby; Martin was free to figure out who he was. Then, the conversation moved on to politics. Wayne was quite conservative at the time, and Martin would say he was a little to the left of Teddy Kennedy. My mother did not care for these discussions and always recommended talking about something else—something not so serious.

Mom was happy to have the three of us together on this day, but I knew she was thinking, too, about her other child. The one who was not among us. The one who was always thought about on holidays but was never spoken about: Pamela Sue.

After dinner, once the dishes were washed, dried, and put away, we took our coffee into the living room and relaxed. Robin had lots of things to share with us, and both of my children were happy to listen to their cousin. My mother disappeared into the library and emerged with a video cassette tape. She had magically pieced together several old reels of film taken with an ancient movie camera. I was surprised to see this camera and that they had even acquired it to begin with, as they were not the type to splurge on things like that. I was grateful that they had, though, knowing that having our home videos on a VCR cassette made it possible to view them without dragging out the projector, which worked inconsistently and tested the limits of its viewers' attention spans.

Today, we waited with anticipation as my mother loaded up the tape, not knowing at all what might be about to appear on the screen. We adults hadn't seen these movies for many years and not once before on the television screen. My two children and niece had never seen them at all.

Everyone settled in and prepared for the premier showing of the Avery Family Archives, and before we knew it, the screen was alive with motion pictures of my older brother and me when we were young. The reactions of our children, who had never seen these videos before, were hysterical. Watching our appearance on film, they were seeing the unimaginable— their parents as children, little people just like them.

The next scenes to appear had been taken outside of our home. Another little person came across the screen—a girl with soft brown hair, cut in the same pixie style as mine, and big blue eyes above a sad sort of smile. This little girl was my sister, Pamela Sue, who was born when I was two years old. While my children had heard me talk about Pam and even seen a few pictures of her, this was to be the first and only opportunity for them to see her as a child and how she was then.

The laughter and conversation ceased as we all watched her move independently across the screen in her walker. She waved her hands and made soft, contented sounds as she strolled easily across the linoleum floor. The room became uncomfortably silent. And here it was—that familiar feeling that had been with me for so long—like feeling homesick, only I wasn't away from home.

We watched as our family pet, a black labrador with the very original name of Blackie, moved carefully and protectively beside her, appearing apprehensive about the filming. I could remember, or at least remember being told, how much this dog had seemed to have a sixth sense about Pammy, as we called her. He seemed to know that there was something very fragile about her, and he rarely left her side. He was protective of me and my brother, too, but there was a very special connection between this dog and Pam. There were even several times when a friend or relative stopped by and reached for her and Blackie appeared between them for reassurance that it was all right—that Pammy was in no danger of harm. Blackie was a therapy dog long before dogs were recognized for their abilities to connect with certain people who needed them.

Looking around the room, I tried to imagine what was going through the minds of everyone in my family. Even my children, as young as they were, did not ask the questions I thought they might ask. They simply accepted the first answer when they asked, "Who is that girl?" and I answered, "That's my little sister, Pammy."

Nothing else was said. Looking at Wayne, I had no idea what, if anything, he had said to Robin about Pam. When I met his eyes, they told me nothing more, only that he was uncomfortable. Over the years of facing emotions too overwhelming to express, we had learned to read each other easily when we looked into each other's eyes. But, this time, the silence was too much. Martin went to the kitchen to grab a snack before returning. He was uncomfortable, too.

Thankfully, the scene on the screen changed to the local swimming pool and everyone lightened up a bit as we watched me and Wayne showing off our aquatic skills. The footage was brief, but there we were, along with our good family friends. The girls in the swimming pool were all wearing bathing caps, something our kids were unfamiliar with. Everyone shared their commentary about our diving skills and how silly we looked. The children were giggling.

I remembered very well the desire to jump off the diving board and into the eleven-foot part of the pool—the deepest. I was transported back to walking on the low diving board with confidence, trying not to think about how deep the water was. When I reached the end of the board, I leaned over, putting my arms out in front of me and one hand on top of the other, and executed what I imagined was the perfect dive. No one told me otherwise. I could still feel it.

Now, observing that moment again on the screen, it was less than stellar. Since this film captured just a moment or two in time, it was difficult to imagine the progress I had made before I conquered the high diving board that day.

I felt my feet slowly climb the ladder. At least once with

every step, I considered chickening out and going back down. But that would be very hard to do with a line of kids waiting for the same opportunity I was in the middle of taking—not only to compete at the dive but to have it captured on film.

Standing up there, I tried telling myself that it wasn't any different than the low board. That just like on the low board, I would just walk (somewhat clumsily) to the end and, after summoning all my courage, jump into the water below. So, in I went, sinking almost to the bottom of the pool before I felt myself rising back up to the surface. Once I broke through, I felt victorious, like I had just won a competition.

Now, watching the scene unfold before me, I realized that as much as I wanted to be proficient at both swimming and diving, I fell short of my own expectations, a tendency that would continue into my adulthood whenever I approached a new challenge: how awkward I would feel even when trying to move naturally. Watching my almost-seven-year-old self was almost like watching my own daughter, her mannerisms and movements nearly identical to mine, though I think she became more confident. It always astounded me how great a role genetics play in making us who we are.

Even though Pam was no longer on screen, I thought about her once again. I thought about how she should have been showing off her diving skills as well but never had the chance. Thinking of how much she missed out on and how this showing of the video was impacting me, feelings surfaced that I hadn't been aware of for many years. Thankfully, the camera crew left the swimming pool, making way for the next scene.

Suddenly, we were observing the backyard of my grandparents' home, which we visited often. Unfortunately, this video, too, brings up some difficult emotions. In it, it appears increasingly difficult for my mother to physically manage Pam.

Several years have passed, and both my parents look sad and tired. My grandparents look uncomfortable, my brother looks self-conscious, and we all attempt to look and move "naturally." Looking back, I realized that repeated attempts to look and move naturally became the blueprint for my family. If you were to observe us even today, you would find the same awkward movements. It is like we are watching our surroundings, watching others watching us, never quite knowing what to do. I call it the "Avery spin."

In this scenario, I was the one who was taking responsibility—to distract, to be the entertainer, making faces and exaggerating my walk, trying desperately to take away the sadness on the faces of those around me I loved so much. I seem to have thought I was much older, but I was only eight years old. I knew that because Pam was still there. That is how old I was when she went to Custer. She was just six.

The silence in the room, interrupted only by the occasional voices of my children, became overwhelming once again as those who knew sat in silent recognition of the fact that this was shortly before Pam was admitted to Custer State Hospital, where she would live for many years. Once she left our home, in fact, she did not return.

It felt as if the pain of that time was with us once again or, perhaps, that it had never really left us. We continued to sit in contemplation as homecoming parades, birthday parties, and family vacations moved across the screen, none of them showing Pam. From that point on, just like in the videos, she was a prominent absence in all of our lives.

At the end of the home movie, it was time to bundle up and return home. Like many other times, I longed to stay there with my kids. It had not been long since my divorce, and going back to an empty house was still difficult at times. As I imagined all parents do, I hoped that even the difficult decisions I'd made were right for my children.

We said goodbye to Wayne and Robin, promising to see them at Christmas. Martin would be home for a few days, so I told him he needed to come over to our house before he left again for school. I hugged my mom a little bit tighter than I might have if we hadn't chosen this activity, and my dad seemed to be deciding whether what we had watched was a good idea or not as he gathered up the garbage from dinner and took it out to my parents' shop. He was gone for a while. Longer than it would have taken to leave the garbage there.

When we returned home, my children had many questions about Pam. Where was she when Grandma was taking pictures at the pool? Where did she go after that? Why didn't she live with you? And the big question: Why didn't you tell me I had an aunt? We talked for a long time.

After my children went to bed, I sat down with my journal and wrote down my feelings about that evening, the memories of that period of time, and the pain that had returned. I was so surprisingly aware that as a family, we never really talked about Pam. It wasn't that any kind of declaration had been made. My parents had never told us *not* to bring her up. But I think my brother and I were always aware of the sadness, and sometimes anger, that was awakened whenever we did.

As the thoughts poured out onto the pages of my journal, I quickly realized that part of what was making me so uncomfortable was that even as I watched myself and everyone else interact with Pam on video, I couldn't find an actual memory of her being at home. Not one single memory of that time came to me. I have always found this puzzling and frustrating, considering all of the other things I remember from even earlier years. Even childhood friends of mine can talk specifically about her—where her crib was, for instance. Writing about this in my journal, I wondered if others whose siblings were placed in institutions experienced similar feelings. I grew curious about the experiences of other families. While my memories were limited, my feelings were still powerful. So I began to write, to share what I could recall and the feelings I had never stopped feeling. To remember Pam and to bring her presence back into our home.

When I was born, you were happy to see me. You were all anxious to take me home, where I would be loved and start my life.

But soon, I saw how your expressions changed when you were with me, and you talked quietly about some things I could not do.

It seemed like maybe you didn't want me there. Where in this world could I belong?

- Barb Avery-Sterud

BEGINNINGS

The course of my life was changed on November 27, 1960, when my sister, Pamela Sue, was born. I had been not quite two years old—and my brother, Wayne, nearly six—when she arrived. When I think of Pamela today, it is difficult to imagine how my life would have been—could have been—without her. I think everyone has markers along their life's journey, situations they refer to as "the moment." The one when the path took a life-changing turn.

I often lingered near our mother at the kitchen table as she sat for coffee with two of my aunts, so the way this day started out was nothing unusual. I grabbed a Rice Krispies bar and migrated into the living room to find something to watch on television. Saturday morning, so maybe the Jetsons? The Flintstones? Before long, I could hear my mother and aunts talking very quietly from the other room. I was seven years old by now, so they tried to keep quiet whenever they brought up things I wasn't supposed to hear. But that didn't mean it always worked. The hushed tones only prompted me to listen more attentively. I went back in the kitchen, noticing my mom had tears in her eyes.

"When Pammy was born, there were problems," my mom explained when she saw me in the doorway. "That's all we are talking about. You don't need to worry—I'll be alright."

"What problems?" I insisted.

Seeing I wasn't going to go away, my mother and aunts told me the story—the same one that, years later, I would come to share in much the same way with my own children. While parts of the story have likely been lost or told just a little bit differently over time, it is her story, nonetheless.

"The doctor and the nurses didn't listen to your mom," Aunt Audrey explained. "She knew her baby was ready to be born, but they didn't believe her."

"Why didn't they believe her?" I asked.

"We really don't know," my mother said. "But I knew she was ready to be born. Maybe they thought they knew better than me, but they didn't."

My mom was in labor, she told me, when my dad took her to the hospital. The nurses checked her into her room and did what they needed to in order to prepare, but they kept saying, "It's too soon. The doctor isn't even here yet."

But, knowing she was already very close to delivering when she went into the hospital, their reassurances did little to comfort her. For reasons unknown, her knowledge of what was happening in her own body was not taken seriously by anyone at the hospital. Perhaps they assumed this was her first baby since they didn't know her or have any records of either me or Wayne, who had been born under very different circumstances in Seattle. For whatever reason, even though my mother knew full well what her body was telling her, she was disregarded.

Finally, she insisted the nurse check her. "I want you to

check," she explained, "Because I know this baby is coming, whether you believe me or not." When she did, the nurse was surprised to find the baby was indeed crowning. Still, the doctor was not there.

Another nurse quickly tried to reach the doctor again. There were two stories that were told about why he was so hard to reach. One was that he was playing golf and didn't think it would be necessary for him to come to the hospital any time soon. The other was that he was out flying his airplane. I don't know which—if either—was true, but, either way, it did not change what happened.

My parents had gotten married in 1953, and, soon after, they moved from their small community of Tulare, South Dakota, to the city of Seattle, Washington. My mother's sister, Esther, lived there with her husband and their children, and my father was quickly able to find work there too, even after my Uncle Jim had cautioned him that jobs were very hard to come by. Circumstances surrounding the birth of babies in the mid-fifties, especially in big cities like Seattle, included hospital brochures that clearly laid out expectations for mothers and fathers and their very different roles during this exciting event. Mothers were sedated and kept in "twilight sleep," and fathers were not allowed to be present at all during the birthing process. They were given explicit instructions as to where they needed to stand and at what time in order to "catch a glimpse" of the babies as they were being carried from the nursery to their mothers.

Guidelines were strictly adhered to, and there was no free time for mothers to be with their babies outside of what was dictated by their feeding schedule, which varied depending on whether babies were bottle- or breast-fed. At the Swedish Hospital, where my brother and I were born, mothers were not awake as babies were brought into the world. They would awake from their "twilight sleep" to the news about their baby girl or boy, a practice that had become commonplace across many states since the 1920s.

Before the 1900s, any knowledge of childbirth came from women, kin, and midwives. However, once the medical profession began to organize into the institution it has become, this knowledge shifted into the hands of doctors, who were, of course, men. Home births had once been normal, everyday events, but medical intervention now regarded them as pathologized forms of childbirth. Textbooks were written for obstetrics, which led to more hospitals being built and the delivery process itself changing.

Dr. Joseph DeLee, who wrote one of these textbooks, believed that few women were harmed by the typical process of childbirth, and he pushed for doctors to be in control over women's labor and delivery. In line with this emerging industry trend, women could be sedated at the start of labor and awakened with no memory of the process. Dilation could even take place manually during this twilight sleep. With the help of episiotomies, forceps, and medications administered to contract the uterus and give the doctors time for the procedure and subsequent repair work, babies could be born with little active participation necessary from the mother, sedated with a combination of morphine and scopolamine, or Devil's Breath, which guaranteed the doctor could maintain total control until the process was over.

By the 1960s, when Pam was born, this patriarchal practice had lost favor, and my mother had nothing to prepare her for the birthing experience that would come, since, for her first two deliveries, she had been asleep. "When the nurse was checking me, I knew something was wrong," my mother said. "She held Pammy back in the birth canal."

She and both of my aunts were crying as she continued, recalling that she knew my father was pacing back and forth in the hallway, probably stepping outside for the occasional cigarette. After their previous childbirth experiences in Seattle, where he hadn't been allowed in with my mother at all, here, he wasn't sure what his role was. He didn't know about my mother's fear or what ultimately happened during the birth.

The nurse continued holding my sister back in the birth canal, physically preventing her from naturally exiting, until the doctor finally arrived. When he did, Pamela Sue was born, and it was immediately clear that she had been deprived of oxygen. They went to work on her, trying to get her to breathe, and eventually, she did, crying out to announce her arrival. My sister was born, and the doctor announced that she was a beautiful, healthy baby. The damage that had been done was not yet evident.

The fact that Pamela was likely to have serious consequences from the oxygen deprivation in the first moments of her life seemed to remain in the shadows. Her baby picture was even entered in a local "most beautiful baby" contest, and she won for having the prettiest smile. Pamela Sue certainly met that criteria with her bright eyes and the way she held her head up independently. I know what babies and toddlers with profound cognitive delays and the complications that come with these delays often look like, and the photos of my sister do not tell the same story. The photo and others like it haunt me to this day.

During those early years, I remember asking questions in an effort to understand what was wrong with Pam. Why couldn't she talk? Why couldn't she walk? How could she learn to walk and talk? Why was everyone so quiet whenever they came to visit and observed her? Why did everyone seem sad? I remember getting answers involving Pam being "sick," and that because of her sickness, she had seizures, which was why she couldn't walk or talk. I'm sure this was the only explanation my parents thought I could understand at that point. But, to me, with little experience of the world around me, I thought that if someone were sick, that meant they would eventually get well.

The years from my sister's birth to the major defining event in all our lives—when she was institutionalized—are somewhat disconnected in my mind. Between those two monumental events were many doctors' appointments, physical therapy appointments, evaluations to understand why she wasn't walking, and eventually braces, in hopes of assisting her ability to do so. All of these appointments strengthened my belief, and hope, that she was going to get better. When I realized she wasn't, I wanted to understand why.

Once she was taken away and I got older, I continued wondering why. I had questions regarding what the experts were calling autism and what the trained staff at Custer State Hospital were doing with Pamela every day that still didn't result in any change or improvement with the help of their interventions. I read everything I could find about my sister's disability, and I was always hoping to see a difference in her. I knew that if I did, it would settle my worries about something similar happening to me.

When I was old enough to pursue my own research, I read *Dibs in Search of Self* by Virginia Axline, a story about a young boy whose family and educators believe he has emotional and cognitive disabilities. Dibs does not talk or play and seems to be locked away in his own prison until he embarks on a year-long journey with play therapy, which unlocks the doors to it. Reading this made me hopeful, even though his diagnosis was very different from Pamela Sue's. I reread this book many times and constantly thought about how even some of the simpler elements of play therapy could have helped Pam. Had we known that, could we have kept her at home with us?

I read *Son-Rise* by Barry Neil Kaufman about his son, who had been diagnosed with autism. Kaufman and his wife became their son's teachers and later went on to establish the Autism Treatment Center of America with a curriculum for other parents of children with autism. These resources were unfortunately not available in the early years of my parents raising Pamela Sue.

My search for answers has stayed with me ever since. When I accompanied my father on a visit to the Mayo Clinic for an evaluation in 2002, I browsed one of the bookstores in Rochester, and a particular book literally fell off the shelf and landed by my feet. Always a believer in signs and signals from the universe, I picked it up. It was *The Normal One: Life with a Difficult or Damaged Sibling*, written by Jeanne Safer, PhD. Like Featherstone's book, *A Difference in the Family*, which I had read when I was in college, it resonated with me, one of those books you put down only because there are tears in your eyes. I was surprised to find someone else who shared similar experiences and felt so many of the feelings I had struggled with over the years.

Dr. Safer writes about something she calls the Caliban Syndrome, which she proposes is typical of all children who have a sibling with a disability. The syndrome alludes to Shakespeare's *The Tempest*, which tells the story of the fraught relationship between Caliban, who is described as a dark and troubled figure, and his sister, Miranda. Unlike Caliban, Miranda is extremely bright and successful at most things she attempts.

Safer describes the symptoms of this syndrome as something that affects everyone differently but that no one escapes from. They include:

Prematurity: Being very mature; grown-up; capable of handling situations beyond what is typical for their age

Survivor guilt: Guilt about being better off than the disabled sibling and able to celebrate accomplishments that the sibling cannot; being prone to anxiety, self-sabotage, and the idea that any personal success heightens the failure of the disabled sibling

Compulsion to achieve: Wanting to excel at everything; displaying perfectionism; fearing failure; being unable to relax and enjoy life

Fear of contagion: Worry about "catching" what the sibling has; always looking for abnormalities in oneself; thinking one has either nothing or everything in common with their sibling

Standing in the bookstore, these descriptors brought me to tears. I was overwhelmed by the accuracy of my own feelings described in Safer's book. As I read her descriptions, I checked all the boxes. I was more mature than other kids my age. Siblings, especially females, often accept too much responsibility for their disabled sibling, moving into the role of caregiver without protest. My brothers and I all carried with us this characteristic—not necessarily in all areas but definitely in some that were significant. I remember feeling very protective, even as a three- or four-year-old child, including of my brother, four years older than me. I had a recurring dream, always the same, where my brother had fallen into a deep hole in our yard and I couldn't get him out. I would run to my parents but couldn't get their attention. My brother would cry from the dark hole he had fallen into, and I was unable to rescue him. The dream never had a different outcome; I was powerless to make things better.

Sometimes, I was praised for being mature and able to talk things through when others were upset. When I was about twelve years old, I was a Girl Scout attending an overnight camp. We had to set up our tents and learn basic skills like some simple cooking, including campfire stew, a delicious browned hamburger and vegetable soup.

When we all were settling into our tents, one of my friends

started talking about being angry with her mom for dying and leaving her and her sister alone with their father. Recently, their father had remarried, and while his new wife was nice and cared deeply for her stepchildren, in our Girl Scout tent in the dark, my friend's tears flowed. I responded with counseling skills beyond my years, explaining that her mother had died of cancer and that she didn't leave her because she wanted to. She loved her children and would probably want them to give this new person a chance. The next day, one of the adult leaders took me aside and told me she had heard our conversation and was impressed with how I helped my friend.

Survivor guilt is complicated. I was happy to be healthy and that I didn't have to go away and live somewhere far away from my family, but my brother and I still felt guilty. We were frequently reminded that my sister had left for our sake and, when we didn't live up to expectations, that the decision had been so we could have a better life. There were times we didn't hold up our part of the bargain.

Safer describes a compulsion to achieve, another aspect I can relate to. I always worked very hard at school, wanting to please my parents and make them proud of me and, therefore, less sad about Pam. I did well in school and won the award for reading the most books every year. Had there been awards for being a friend, helping others, or showing empathy before I even knew what the word was, I would have received those, too.

I was in elementary school at a time when many things were happening in education, and some of the ideas worked great for me. I worked my way through the various levels of school, mastering the information, taking my quizzes and tests, and moving on to what came next. My parents must have been proud of my accomplishments, but my efforts didn't seem to do anything to reduce their sadness. So I kept trying.

I was an avid reader from the very beginning. Books were magical to me. Academic achievement was equally important to me because it allowed me to demonstrate that there was no problem here. That everything was fine. But I didn't dare let my guard down. I thought that whatever sickness Pam might have would come to me. If Pam could be so sick, then maybe I could be also. Fear of contagion means that children without a disability often worry about somehow being susceptible to getting one ourselves.

Safer described my childhood fears well: "No one with an abnormal sibling has a normal childhood. Consciously or unconsciously, every intact sibling is haunted by the fear of catching the disability. They feel tormented by the compulsion to compensate for their parents' disappointments by having no problems and making no demands, and they are often unaware of the massive external and internal pressure to pretend that nothing was amiss."

I began to feel that this world may not be such a safe place. If my parents could not do all the things they seemed to be capable of to make my sister well, how could I trust them to take care of me?

I am the Voice of the Voiceless
Through me, the dumb shall speak
Till the world's deaf ear be made to hear
The wrongs of the wordless weak.

Oh, shame on the mothers of mortals
Who do not stoop to teach
The sorrow that lies in dear, dumb eyes
The sorrow that has no speech.
From street, from cage, from kennel
From stable and from zoo
The wall of my tortured kin proclaims the sin
Of the mighty against the frail.
But I am my brother's keeper
And I shall fight their fight
And speak the word for beast and bird
Till the world shall set things right.

- Ella Wheeler Wilcox

PLEASE DON'T
EAT THE DAISIES

A bandonment runs in my family. There must be a kinder way to state that, but it is true. I have tried to find words to explain what I mean exactly by abandonment, the state of being left helpless and without protection. It can be described in many ways; perhaps this is one of the reasons my sister's story is important to tell.

In the context of my immediate family, Pamela Sue was the ultimate example of this. She was born, she smiled, she sang her little song, and then she was gone from our lives, just as surely as if she had died. In fact, it might have been easier if she had—a death in the family at least often results in the family coming together to grieve, in public and in private. In a healthy family, memories are shared during these difficult times. Sharing is encouraged. Comfort is provided to one another, and tears are allowed to flow. Friends and relatives come to offer support, and the memories that wash over them are put out in the open, often accompanied by hugs and community.

But Pam did not die. She was sent away, placed in an institution for individuals with "mental retardation." And then everyone had to act like nothing had happened.

Wayne and I were in our spots on the living room floor, waiting for *Please Don't Eat the Daisies* to begin. It was Sunday evening, and we didn't want to miss the new television show about a couple living in an old house in New York with their four rambunctious boys, a live-in maid, and an enormous Old English sheepdog. We each had a blanket, five ounces of Coca-Cola—we always shared one ten-ounce bottle—and Blackie was stretched out beside us.

Our living room had a red couch, a matching chair, and easy-to-clean linoleum flooring—which was likely why we were permitted the Coke for this Sunday evening ritual. A large picture window facing north showed the highway that went by our house. It was a perfectly normal evening in front of the television until my parents came in and said they had something important to talk to us about. My brother and I exchanged looks—we knew it was important because these deliberate family meetings were unfamiliar to us. Wayne shut off the television and sat up to listen.

My father started the conversation. "You both know that we've been taking Pammy to lots of doctors' appointments lately."

We nodded in agreement. We had not gone to any of the appointments and didn't understand what exactly they were for, nor were we aware of the conversations or specific consultations that must have been taking place prior to this moment. All we had was a vague idea of Pam's "sickness" and the hope that a solution was being worked on.

"What did you find out?" Wayne asked.

"Well," our father continued. "They had much to say about

the kinds of support they believed would help Pam the most. And that she needs more support than what we can give her at home."

"What kind of support?" I asked, beginning to feel a little defensive.

"Extra support," my mother added. "From people who are really good at caring for children like her, who have seizures like she does. It seems like they've been getting worse lately," she added. "The sad part is that she will have to go somewhere else to get that support."

"You mean like school?" my brother asked. "She would still come home at the end of the day, right?"

My dad's eyes were wet with tears. He explained that school couldn't take care of her because she couldn't walk or talk. She would have to go stay somewhere far away from Redfield, and she would be leaving before the end of the month, but we could go and see her.

Seeing this sadness in my parents, my eyes also filled with tears. They were trying so hard to make this positive, but what I felt was not positive at all.

I looked back and forth at them. "Why can't she just stay here? We can do more to help her. We can spend more time with her and do other things so Mom won't be so busy."

But it was no use. At the end of the month, just as promised, Wayne and I stayed with our good friends, and our parents left to take Pam to Custer. They seemed more sad on this day than ever before, and I felt sick to my stomach as I said goodbye to them and Pam. As they went out the door, I'm not sure I fully understood that they would be coming back without my sister. I shouted out, "Have fun!" and knew right away that I had said the wrong thing, but it was too late.

The rationale for her having to leave our family and go to

an institutional setting, I later learned, was based in part on an increase in seizure activity that could not be curtailed. The physical demands the episodes would have placed on my mother, who was very small in stature but also very strong, must have been hard. My parents were active in the Association for Retarded Children at the time, and it may have come up at one of these meetings. On top of that, there was no opportunity to provide education for Pamela at the time— the Education for the Handicapped Act, later known as Public Law L94-142, would have allowed her to go to school. But that was still ten years down the road.

My grown-up mind and the expertise I've accrued in special education can understand the rationale. As an adult who has worked in the special education field my entire career now, I can fill in many of the blanks that my earlier self lacked, but I will never have a fully accurate timeline for how my parents came to understand the true nature of my sister's disabilities.

Before she left, Pam was able to feed herself crackers and other finger foods. She made eye contact and liked to watch whatever was happening around her. She had a funny little noise she made, which we quickly called her "happy sound."

What she did not do was meet developmental milestones for language development. Between the ages of one and two, normal language development includes using many words, starting to name pictures in books, asking "what," "who," and "where" questions, and putting two words together, such as "more apple" or "mommy book." Receptively, children between these ages are able to name a few body parts when asked to and begin to point out images when given the corresponding word.

The difference between what knowledge was available to new parents then and now is remarkable. Resources are available from physicians who can make referrals to the Birth to Three program and others like it. Nowadays, parents are contacted by someone from the B-3 team, who observes the child and does some initial assessments before enrolling them in the program. Once in, teams of speech-language pathologists and occupational and physical therapists determine what the greatest needs are and begin working with the family in their home, starting with the area where the biggest delay is present. Others are added as needed. The determined techniques are modeled for parents, who learn how to most effectively interact with and care for their children along the way. In my experience with special education, parents look forward to these visits from providers and are forever grateful for the bonds they help develop both inside and outside of the immediate family.

I can only imagine what outcomes could have been possible for Pamela and my parents if such measures of support had been available to them when they were in need. But, unfortunately, they didn't exist. People in these circumstances had to figure it all out on their own.

A question that many people ask is why Pamela had to go all the way to Custer State Hospital when Redfield State Hospital and School were right there where we lived. The answer my parents were given was that RSHS was no longer taking individuals who were non-ambulatory. That seemed to answer the question for me at the time. However, I later developed my own explanation. I'd imagine it would have been exceptionally hard on my parents to know their daughter was right in the same community, so close by and yet out of our reach. This was consistent with the institution's viewpoint, which maintained that families benefited from not remaining involved in their child's day-to-day activities. In their eyes, distance made the transition easier for all involved. The staff who were advising my parents told them she would still be part of her family—just a very long way from what had been her home.

Much of my life was shaped by the transition that began on that Sunday evening in front of the television. Years of research show that siblings of children with disabilities—and especially sisters—often develop a strong sense of compassion for others and make helping others their life's work. This was definitely the case for me. I can remember feeling my heart break when classmates would make fun of children who were different.

When I was in the fifth grade, I was standing by a bookcase in Mrs. Angela Eining's classroom when an incident on the playground caught my attention. There, on the other side of the window, my friend Elizabeth was being called a retard. Hearing her being treated like that brought me to tears, and I made up my mind that I was going to do something for "handicapped people," to somehow make life better for them. My use of the word handicapped is intentional, as this was long before the realization of any need for people-first language. Comments and taunts about "acting like a retard" were painful for me to hear.

Elizabeth has her own story to tell, but, with her permission, I share it here. Elizabeth's family was unique—unique in the fact that Elizabeth was one of four siblings and the only one without an intellectual disability. Elizabeth's parents both had mild intellectual disability, but my friend would likely disagree with my assessment. She knew she was loved and cared for and that this was what mattered most and proved they were plenty capable—and she is right about this.

Elizabeth's dad worked for the County Highway Department, and her mother in the kitchen of the Redfield State Hospital and School, later named South Dakota Developmental Center.

Both Elizabeth's mother and father worked very hard to get by on what they made, and her mother even worked another job washing dishes at a local café. They were living well below the poverty line, but it certainly wasn't for lack of working.

Elizabeth's two older siblings, Sandy and Katie, and her younger brother, Paul, all fit that era's definition of "mentally retarded." And all three were institutionalized at some point over the course of my friend's childhood. Elizabeth's little brother, Paul, had been taken to live at the State School long before our fifth-grade playground experiences, and Elizabeth's exposure to bullying and taunting never quit. The playground bullies were tenacious, always looking for creative new ways to incorporate "retard" into their name-calling. It never let up. After the school day ended, the older children who lived in the neighborhood followed them home from school to continue the verbal assaults. Now, more than fifty years later, this issue has begun to be addressed by school and community campaigns, with signs and T-shirts that read, "The r-word hurts. Spread the word to end the word." My question is why this is still a topic of discussion more than fifty years later. It was hurtful then, and it remains hurtful now. Why hasn't this already changed? Had it really gone unnoticed by so many until recently? I am still devoting my life to trying to heal myself and others from the damage done by this type of behavior.

Elizabeth was six years old when Paul first went to the Redfield State Hospital and School, as it was named at that time. He was only three years old. Elizabeth didn't know why he had to go away—he had been happy at home. All he did was turn the lights on and off, over and over, and stare into them, laughing and singing silly songs. "He just wanted to be loved and to love us," she has said. He was her baby brother, and she was supposed to protect him. But she had not been able to.

Elizabeth remembers being in the car when Paul was taken away for the first time. She remembers the staff taking his clothes and explaining to her parents that they had to mark them with his name. So they took all of his little white T-shirts and jeans and began writing his name in them as the workers—houseparents, as they were called then—went to get Paul from the car. He was scared and understandably confused, and he fought and cried and screamed as Elizabeth sat quietly and helplessly watching the scene unfold and not understanding why they had to do this to him. He was so scared. She was so scared. Were they going to take her, too?

Her fears were similar to what I had experienced: What did it take for the grown-ups to decide you needed to go away and live somewhere else? If my sibling can't stay at home, what's to say that I can for much longer? We were always one step away from being taken away, just like them.

Sitting in that room, Elizabeth wanted them to stop. She wanted her parents to get back in the car. She wanted them to drive them all back to their house, where he could keep singing silly songs instead of crying like this.

But she was only six years old. What could she do? How could she take it all in? Her parents seemed equally unsure how to manage their desperate son and reacted to him almost like he was in trouble, instructing him to go into the building with the houseparents, who were clearly in charge. As she saw that her parents, too, appeared afraid of these strangers. Elizabeth's throat grew tight. She tried hard not to cry as Paul disappeared behind the doors to his dormitory.

From that day on, every time they brought Paul home for a weekend, that same scene played out upon his return to the center. On one visit, she remembered hearing that if he continued to be uncooperative, he wouldn't get to come home at all any more. So she began quietly whispering to him not to get upset, trying to assure him that he would be okay and that she would keep him safe if he just did what they told him to do. Stopping him from coming home made no sense to her six-year-old mind. And then she reasoned that she'd better not get upset either, or they might make her stay there, too. Witnessing her little brother's abandonment, it was all too easy to imagine herself being sent away in kind.

What she needed was reassurance. Reassurance that Paul was able to settle down once he got into the building. Reassurance that her family would be able to continue to visit him there and take him home when they wanted to. Because her parents were trying desperately to make sense of it themselves and because their circumstances were further complicated by their own intellectual limitations, she never received that.

What my friend and I didn't know was that we were in the midst of major changes beyond either of our personal circumstances. Changes were happening throughout the country, through grassroots movements by the parents of children who were being left out of public education entirely.

During John F. Kennedy's presidency, he became an advocate for people with disabilities when he first learned that his sister, Rosemary, was intellectually disabled. When he went to visit her for the first time, Rosemary had been living in an institution for ten years while her parents tried extremely hard to hide their family secret. The experience of JFK's family led to historic progress being made in the treatment of intellectual disabilities. At that time, most of the more than 400,000 people who were identified as having severe and profound intellectual disabilities required constant supervision, and most of them were held in residential institutions at public expense. JFK's involvement meant major changes in how services were thought of and delivered in the United States. It also cemented a number of perceptions that took decades to prevail. In fact, no one actually required institutionalization. In fact, people could be supported to work. In fact, families could be happy.

It was during this time that more research into the practice of removing individuals from the home began to be done. People began to recognize the deep wounding of parents and families of retarded children being caused at the time. Parents had been encouraged to institutionalize their disabled children early, not to keep pictures of them, not get emotionally attached, and to try their best to forget them and consider having another child instead. Pamela and Paul were both placed right at the time the United States was beginning to figure out that neither children nor adults deserved to be separated from their families. But it would be a long time before the country began to explore alternatives like what the Redfield State Hospital and School developed into, where the facilities included gardens, laundries, and farms where individuals worked and took pride in their ability to contribute.

Many people still bought into the idea that adults and children with disabilities should be kept somewhere else, separate from the community. One time, I walked into the local five-and-dime store to look around for whatever I might purchase with my three quarters. A Redfield State Hospital and School employee was in the store with a small group of boys. The boys were looking around, obviously enjoying all that glittered. When I walked to the counter with my purchases, I could see that the store clerk did not want to wait on one of the boys, and she made some comments that she didn't quite bother to keep under her breath.

The caretaker asked the clerk if there was a problem, and she replied, "We don't need these kids coming around here, making noises and walking through the store. They were put in the hospital for a reason, and that's where they should stay."

Surprised by the blatantly judgemental thoughts I overheard, I kept my reaction to myself, afraid that if I responded, I would be challenging an adult, and adults were in charge. Standing outside the store, I thought about what would make a person feel this way about these innocent children. Certainly, people come into this store with children who make noises and run around the aisles. Why was it acceptable for her to talk so meanly about these boys?

Unfortunately, this type of response has remained all too commonplace. The widespread institutionalization of years past removed children with disabilities from their homes, families, and society for generations—it's no wonder the majority of people have still never been exposed to or learned how to interact with them. Many people still feel this is the way things should be.

My fear is that the world may be willing to revert back to these old, oppressive practices. The Education for All Handicapped Children Act (EHA) went into effect when it was signed by Gerald Ford in 1975. This was reauthorized in 1990 and became the Individuals with Disabilities Education Act (IDEA). This revision focused more on helping families plan for transition after high school and an emphasis on students attending their own community schools.

Prior to the Education for All Handicapped Children Act and the revisions that have followed, there were restrictions on children with disabilities being accepted in a public school setting. Criteria for these individuals were determined in consideration of several questions: Were these individuals productive? Were they burdensome to others? Were they capable of socializing? Were they potty-trained? Could they ever contribute to their communities? If we revert to making these kinds of decisions based on questions like these, what would stop us from stepping backward on a grander scale?

Today, my hope is that, as a nation, we have more information to support why it would be wrong to take the position once more that institutionalization is the best we can do. However, I am also aware that keeping people with significant disabilities home is often a very expensive situation for families.

I need to clarify here that there are mini-institutions today that differ greatly from the large institutional mode. There are group homes and specialized programs that allow children to sleep in beds in rooms that they share with maybe one or two other children rather than in a huge dayroom. They provide learning and therapeutic interventions for the inhabitants and aren't treated as a forever placement.

These modern options are driven more by a child's Individual Education Program (IEP) team made up of parents, teachers, related service providers, and individuals who had a part in evaluating the student for evaluation or re-evaluation. The goal of the IEP is always to ensure that the child is being served in the least restrictive environment (LRE). This is one of the main guiding principles in the Individuals with Disabilities Education Act.

Whether Pamela went to Custer or to Redfield, she did not have the option to stay at home with her family. In the years when my parents made the decision to place her, when they were devastated and alone and needed support, it wasn't there. It made many people uncomfortable. My mother experienced this when she went to a meeting of United Methodist Women and talked about the decision to place Pam, the advice they had been given, and how hard it was on all of us. After an awkward silence, the meeting chair promptly got the group back on track to decide what their annual project would be and how much money they were going to devote to missions that year. My mother left feeling hurt and embarrassed about having brought it up in the first place. She had not been heard and realized that in this sacred space, subjects like that were better left unshared. So my mother stuffed all of her feelings, understanding that, sadly, she would not find support there.

I have never known whether both of my parents believed Custer State Hospital would be the best plan for my sister or whether one of them pushed for it more than the other. In my heart of hearts, I believed that if either of them had advocated for the decision, it would have been my father. Time and time again, while I was growing up, he expressed the *hell* he had gone through taking Pam to Custer, following it up with a not-so-subtle reminder that the decision had been made "for the sake of the other children."

I may never know the answer to this question, but I can say with grown-up certainty that they both did exactly what they thought was their only option. They made a decision that they had been led to believe by professionals would be best for everyone at the time. They followed through with that decision and walked through the rest of their lives working hard, living day by day, and going through the motions. But, in many ways, they both disappeared. My parents did their work and followed their daily routines enough to keep things on an even keel, but once Pam had left our home, what she'd left behind was much silence and little joy.

We are not in control
of what lessons
others are here
to learn.
their journey
wasn't ever ours to take.

- Danielle Doby

HISTORY
REPEATS ITSELF

A bandonment has been a theme that has traveled through my family for generations and appeared in different ways long before Pamela Sue came into the world. In an effort to understand my father's reactions and decision-making regarding Pam, I had to look at the relationships within his family of origin and how they may have been impacted by another Avery family experience with disabilities or mental illness.

Lloyd was my father's oldest brother, twelve years his senior. I had learned about my uncle throughout my childhood in bits and pieces—that he went to live at the Yankton State Hospital in his late teens and never returned, aside from the occasional visit home. Lloyd was also very bright and artistic, but he had many mental struggles and anger management problems. As a teenager, he put his fist through a window, the event that ultimately led to his placement.

Every once in a great while, when I was young, we would go

to my grandparents' home in a smaller town ten miles away and sit awkwardly in their tiny living room while an adult we did not know sat there with us. This was my Uncle Lloyd.

My grandparents' home was magical to me as a child. It seemed so big then but was actually broken up into very small rooms. We always entered using the steps that passed my grandmother's yellow rose bush. The other entrance to the house was through an enclosed porch on the opposite side. It was always a treat to sit out there drinking lemonade and watching the cars drive by on the gravel road, which, in this small town, didn't happen very frequently.

My grandmother, Emma Wilhelmina VorderBerg-Avery, always greeted us as we entered. Her house often smelled of homemade cookies and breads, but she had other treats as well, like the round, thick mints that always adorned her table. The pink ones tasted like Pepto Bismol, but the white ones were much better. The Walnut Crush candy bars—fascinating only because they were the one candy bar my brother and I never saw anywhere else—were wrapped in orange paper and made of fluffy marshmallow nougat and slivered walnuts dipped in dark chocolate. My grandmother believed that no meal was complete without dessert. For planned family dinners, she made amazing chocolate cake and all kinds of pies imaginable. Dessert was always there, even if it was just the type of jello and fruit concoction they always seemed to serve at funerals.

There was a furnace grate on the floor between the dining room and living room. No matter how much I was cautioned about not standing on it because it got really hot, nothing felt better than placing your cold toes against the warm metal after coming in from the winter snow. Standing there as my toes defrosted, I let my imagination wander, envisioning what might be under the grate. Were there people down there in the basement? Where did they come from? Why exactly was everyone so vigilant about avoiding the grate? Could it set us on fire?

Another mystical object was my grandfather's vintage ashtray, a couple of feet tall and about ten inches in diameter with a wrought iron base and the tray at the top. A mechanism on its side slid the tray open to allow the ashes to drop into a deeper receptacle. This object became my focal point during the very uncomfortable setting of Uncle Lloyd's visit.

Even though he could talk, Lloyd did not speak during this visit. He just sat there silently, looking every bit as uncomfortable as everyone else in the room. My mother kept busy, checking if anyone wanted coffee and helping my grandma with her guests. My other uncle, Gene, preoccupied himself with his young son, Allen, keeping him out of harm—most likely away from the furnace grate. He walked with a cigarette and a small ashtray in hand. All the while, I searched my mind for something meaningful to say and kept coming up empty. At one point, Grandma sat down and began rubbing her knees with her hands.

"What's the matter, Ma?" my dad asked, "Are your knees sore? They look like they're hurting."

At last, something to talk about!

"No, they don't hurt," Grandma answered him, offering a smile. Then, things became quiet again.

The few times we participated in these visits, the room filled with a sense of sadness and heaviness that I couldn't name at the time. Years later, I can. The pervasive cloud that engulfed every single one of us was *shame*.

Shame was the reason we never talked about Lloyd, the reason no one explained anything about him as if he were simply an uncle visiting from far away. There were few conversations about Lloyd and very little understanding for the family.

He was the family secret of that generation. Even now, there is very little that we know about him.

In the two years following my mother's death in 2016, my father talked more about Lloyd than ever before. He describes the relentless taunting that he and his brother, Eugene, experienced because Lloyd was so different from the other kids. It was tough growing up with Lloyd and tougher still after he went to Yankton. My father was not very descriptive of any specific incidents, but he remembers being embarrassed by his brother's behavior. He described Lloyd as very artistic but unable to control his temper—a description that could fit a significant number of adolescents, then and now. In my recollection, Lloyd was never anything but calm, showing no indications of the angry outbursts that reportedly led to his placement in Yankton.

It is important to recognize that a definite diagnosis was not necessarily something a family would get from a placement at Yankton State Hospital in those days. This is because it really didn't matter why the child was being sent away; the decision had been made that he could not remain at home with his family or in his community, and that was that. People were taken to the state hospitals for many reasons, none of them really explored. When it first opened, Redfield was known by the vague description of "Home for the Feeble-Minded." Often, misunderstood terms like "dementia" were thrown around in lieu of any deeper analysis of the disability and potential treatment options. When in doubt, children would be sent there, medicated there, and maybe, if things went well enough, they would be able to go home for a very awkward visit with their family.

There is a huge problem with this: People are impacted by diagnoses, and diagnoses change with the times. In the education system, a child may be eligible for autism support in the second grade, and because the law outlines when a re-evaluation takes place, he may later lose his eligibility for services. So, does this child have autism? As an adult who has worked with children with disabilities my whole life, I now wonder if Lloyd would have been diagnosed with autism and provided support today.

I can only imagine that when my father married and started his family to find his youngest daughter was born with suspected disabilities, the shame was carried into our house, where it would remain for a very long time. Putting the pieces together with my father's experience growing up with a sibling with a disability, I felt like I understood him a little better. My father, who often seemed distant and angry, must have felt that it was safer to attach a physical symptom to what he was feeling, complaining of headaches and chest pain rather than referring to more deep-rooted emotional distress he may have felt since the childhood issues with his brother Lloyd.

I believe my father has always suffered from generalized anxiety disorder, which was never clinically diagnosed as far as I know. I have mentioned the possibility many times throughout the years, and each time, it has been met with accusations that I was saying he was crazy. A sensitive spot, it seems.

Yet, for years, he suffered from physical and psychological maladies that absolutely stopped him in his tracks, sending him to the hospital. He was always convinced the doctors would find something seriously wrong with him, sure that he was going to have a heart attack by the age of 56, when both of his brothers had died from them. My dad anticipated the same outcome for years.

One time, my father suffered what has since been described as something that sounds like a significant anxiety episode but, at the time, was seen as a mysterious hospitalization. We went to visit him at the hospital and, all together, went for lunch at Frank's Hamburgers—whose claim to fame was their nineteen-cent hamburgers—in Huron, South Dakota. As he sucked in his Pall Mall cigarette, he announced that he was going to "smoke this one down to the nib," as it would be his last. He quit smoking then and there at Frank's 19¢ Hamburgers. He also decided he could no longer continue in the auto body business—paint fumes had been mentioned as a potential trigger for whatever it was that had brought him to the hospital. The next day, he came home. No damage to his heart had been found, and we always wondered if what he had was truly a heart attack.

Dad began to carry nitroglycerin in his pocket, just in case. When I was at Northern State University, I met him and my mother at Perkins for lunch. It was evident that he was feeling really uncomfortable, and he went to the restroom to take nitroglycerin. This happened frequently. Any time he had any bit of chest pain—likely indigestion following a chocolate dessert—he was convinced that it was "the big one."

Many times, my father's anxiety followed news that someone else in the family was struggling with a crisis or illness. Within days, he would also fall very ill. My son's diagnosis of multiple sclerosis at age 23 was followed by an emergency trip to the Mayo Clinic—for my father, not my son, who was dealing with his diagnosis and coming to terms with the challenges he would face. Several doctors had already checked my father over and found nothing wrong, but he woke up and told my mother that if he didn't get to Rochester, he knew he would die. So I drove them to Rochester, my dad lying flat in the back seat the entire way, moaning. As soon as he saw a doctor, he was already showing signs of recovery.

I was in the room when the occupational therapist was asking him questions, which, unbeknownst to him, were part of a dementia assessment. One of them was, "How many children did he have?"

He answered: "Four," the number that included Pamela Sue.

He could not provide all of our names, but he could share plenty about his history of heart problems, which prompted more tests and the same results as always. His heart was just fine from a physiological standpoint, but it was indeed broken.

I was a little boy and I would push you
In your chair—you and I would roll.
In the yard, sweet sunshine dancin'
In the photo, I see a smile.

I look back and think of the distance
I look back—never touched your soul
Who were you then? I'm still askin'.
Not much changed—I still don't know.
Marble met the sun, still it is shining.

Although my own son will never know,
No more vacation in the hills,
No more the bitter lobby cold.
The story ended yesterday.
I've got a picture of a story told.

~ Martin Avery

MISSING HER

After Pam went to Custer, the feeling of sadness, that things were never going to be the same, and an overwhelming sense of loneliness enveloped me. There were no feelings of relief that she was gone, only of abandonment. When I think about being a child, I remember being on my own much of the time.

My earliest memories of my mother, too, are of how sad, exasperated, and exhausted she was. I remember her crying much of the time. Once, I went to stay with my Aunt Lydia and Uncle Ernie on their farm. I didn't know them well, only that they seemed very old. My mother was the youngest of the Walton siblings, and Lydia was the oldest.

My parents were on their way to the Black Hills. I learned later they were going there to meet someone at Custer State Hospital, for they had been told by Redfield State Hospital and School that it might be a better fit for Pam, and they wanted to see it for themselves. My mother called to explain that a winter storm was building and that she was concerned about coming to get us.

"Don't make her come and get you," my aunt sternly said before handing me the phone.

I was relieved to hear my mother's kind voice on the line.

"Hi, honey, how are you?"

"I'm okay. Are you coming to pick me up?"

"We can't, sweetheart. It's snowing really hard where we are, and we can't drive on those roads."

She assured me that they would see me Saturday, but I had no idea what day it was or how many sleeps it would be until then. I was happy she had called but also sad and a little scared that maybe they wouldn't be coming back for me.

A few years before she passed, my mother found some pictures of me and Pam snuggling on the couch together, playing with our cat and smiling happily. In the absence of any clear memories of Pam, these snapshots tell the story of two sisters who shared something special. When Pam went to Custer, I believe I shut down in many ways. Looking back, I don't remember much of anything about home during this time.

What I do remember is Mrs. White and kindergarten and blue mechanical pencils for handwriting lessons and the fact that it was in the little white church across the street from the school. I remember John Long and Elizabeth Dilley. I remember paint smocks and wood floors and coat closets. I remember first grade and Mrs. Burgaard and bringing red fingernail polish to school, spilling it on my white socks, and sitting on the steps with Mrs. Burgaard as I admitted that I had. I remember her kindness.

I remember learning to read and the reading books we used—I can still see them and smell them. I remember the "new" building at school when I started first grade. I remember what Mrs. Geary looked like in second grade. I remember what Miss Walter looked like in third grade and that she smelled like cigarettes, and Miss Marta Small in fourth grade—the best teacher ever. She could see me. She recognized that I was bright and that there were times when I was dissociating and my mind was somewhere else. She knew that I liked to write stories, and there were times when she suggested I write when I didn't seem to be concentrating. She only taught in Redfield for one year before moving to New York, but she rescued me by helping me to realize I could have choices: I could choose to be present. In the fourth grade in public school, she rescued me by giving me a safe place to land.

I took this tactic home, too. When my friends came over, we sometimes took one of the stories I was working on and created and directed plays to pass the time. The room off the living room in our big house on the highway became our playroom. It was there where we had the piano and the large, wooden double doors that opened—an amazing curtain for our stage. We put on plays, pulled everything out that we needed for costumes, and opened the double doors at the start of our performances. My amazing mother allowed us to use items from the cupboards, along with our imaginations, to bring our shows to life.

The playroom piano was old, upright, and somewhat out of tune, but my piano teacher, Mrs. Adrian, marveled at how my chubby little fingers flew over the keys when I played it. When I was younger, I had wanted a piano so badly. I dreamed of one day having one, and, in the meantime, I improvised on TV trays with masking tape keys colored in with black magic marker.

I was determined. I imagined the music I was playing, borrowed beginner piano books from our friends, and practiced every day on my substitute piano. My parents were probably concerned about my skewed sense of reality and decided they'd better buy me the piano before facing the fact that I might have mental issues, too. It sounds humorous, but this is another example of the fear of contagion that Safer describes in her book. My parents had no reason to think I had any learning or mental problems, but maybe they felt like they still needed to be watchful, just in case I started exhibiting potential symptoms.

Connected to the playroom was a small closet with open shelves that was connected to the tiny room no larger than the closet that served as my mother's sewing area. There was only enough room for her sewing machine cabinet and her many fabrics and trimmings. My mother was a talented seamstress who sewed most of her clothes and mine, and I remember listening to her sewing machine whirring as I watched her hands feeding the fabric through the machine, knowing she was creating something amazing. I sought out sounds like that because they brought me comfort.

In all my years, I felt particularly lonely on Sundays, away from school and having the expanse of the whole day stretching out in front of me. Those were the afternoons I often spent in this small space near my mother, listening to the sewing machine and music on the radio.

I think we all were lonely, but we didn't know how to connect, to reach out to each other and be still in the loneliness. Constructed reality tells me the best professional advice available at the time dictated that Pam would be institutionalized—"for the sake of the other children." So we learned early on that talking about Pam was likely to trigger an emotional response, and it became "the silence."

I remember the first of many trips to Custer to visit Pam. They were our annual family vacations, and they started out happily as we headed out in one of the several Volkswagen vans my dad owned throughout the years. Wayne and I would usually go to sleep in the van the night before, so we could get an early start—or maybe it was just exciting to sleep in the van in preparation for vacation, knowing we would wake up to the sounds of my parents talking, to the smell of their coffee, and the possibility that where there was coffee, there may also be our favorite cookies or donuts to go with it.

In the days leading up to our departure, there was a sense of adventure and anticipation. My mother would spend mornings thinking through the grocery list of food to take along, making snacks and baking cookies. Road trips at the time didn't involve pit stops at iconic places to eat, mostly because they weren't available to the degree that they are now. And we were always careful about spending. Looking back, I cannot imagine the economic hardship these trips created for them.

I remember my mother wearing her pedal pushers and a crisp white sleeveless blouse, turning in her passenger-side seat and crawling back to get things from the refrigerator as dad drove, passing out snacks and refilling their coffee cups. Those days of camping involved packing our own food; cooking eggs, bacon, and pancakes on the green Coleman stove; and stopping by roadside parks to eat bologna sandwiches and Fritos corn chips. On our trips out to Custer, I sometimes came very close to feeling happy.

The scenery was sensational. The east side of South Dakota, where we lived, was completely different from the west side with the Black Hills, which felt like the best place in the world to be. Beautiful evergreen trees dotted the mountainsides as far up as the eye could see, and water ran through small brooks, captivating my attention as it moved. At lunchtime, we often found a park close to one of the brooks, and we would wade in the cold water. The water, unlike at most of the lakes I'd seen, was clear enough to see the little rocks at the bottom. It was invigorating, breathing in the fragrances of the trees and feeling the water on our feet as my parents studied the map, trying to find a place nearby for us to set up our campsite. Eventually, they did, and we set up camp at a nice spot in the Black Hills National Forest.

The trip from Redfield to Custer was about 350 miles. It was long, but that was the wonderful thing about traveling in our VW bus. We could always take little rest stops along the way. But the mood and the tone always changed as we got closer and closer to the state hospital. By the time we saw the huge sign on the mountain that read CUSTER, conversation between my parents always grew quiet as we ascended the winding roads of the Black Hills, up the driveway to the Custer State Hospital.

I was excited to see my little sister, but the building she was in was not what I had envisioned. Huge and formidable, it was quite intimidating, especially for a child. The facilities had once been used as the Tuberculosis Sanatorium, and, once tuberculosis was no longer as rampant, they reopened as the Custer State Hospital in 1963.

My mother mentioned that we'd be taking Pam with us to the campsite but explained that she wasn't sure what to expect when we got inside or if we'd even be let into Pam's room along with the adults. As soon as we all entered the building, that became clear as we watched our parents disappear to the floor where my sister resided. Children were not allowed to be in the "wards," as they were called then.

Terminology has changed frequently over the years, wards becoming dormitories, giving the impression that institutionalization is similar to going to camp or being in college. Patients became residents, then clients, then individuals. Changing the descriptors, though, did nothing to change the reality of their lives.

Wayne and I squirmed restlessly on the green vinyl furniture of the huge marble waiting area. We weren't allowed in the wards, but that didn't keep us from seeing the patients—individuals with hydrocephalus, with very large heads and blank stares—as they were wheeled to and from those mysterious places in wheelchairs, walkers, and beds. Nor did it change how frightening it all seemed. Why did anyone think this was an environment for a small child?

Nothing in this environment even tried to be welcoming to families as they visited. Everything was white and antiseptic, the smell of Pine-Sol hanging in the air to cover up the smell of urine. It seemed like we waited forever for our parents, anxiously wondering what might be going on in the different parts of this enormous building we had no access to. In all the times we would visit this place, we were never approached by anyone greeting us or asking if we would like crayons and coloring books. Warm and fuzzy, it was not.

When our parents finally came down with Pam in her walker, the change in our sister was immediately noticeable. Pam was pale and had dark circles under her beautiful eyes. She didn't vocalize in the same way as she had when she was home. She looked sleepy, likely from the medications they were giving her. My parents already looked sad and broken—worn out from even the short time since they disappeared from our sight. That's what I remember the most—the anxiety I felt when I realized just how vulnerable and fragile my parents appeared. They didn't seem to feel any safer or more self-assured than me or my brother.

In moments like these, the origins of the awkward feelings that would become so universal in our family were beginning to develop. The "What are we doing here?" and "How are we supposed to be acting?" and "How should we be feeling under these circumstances?" and "How can we be feeling anything at all when we are so numb?" were questions that would continue to haunt us, even as we never found the answers to them.

After what seemed like an eternity, we were once again in the safety of our VW van. My mother held Pam on her lap, and we squeezed her walker in wherever it could fit. We went back to the campground, which we hadn't had time to explore much before picking Pam up. And now she was there with us, with her walker, which allowed her a bit of independence, but the terrain was different and more difficult than what she was used to. My brother and I enjoyed helping her get around as we explored together.

I watched as my mother attempted to feed Pam little crackers and finger foods. She sat close to her daughter, talking to her soothingly, but Pam wasn't interested in any of the crackers. I could see the despair in my mother's eyes and hear the distress in her voice. She told my dad that Pam was losing skills she had before she had left us. Before, Pam had been able to feed herself these crackers and other finger foods. Now, she didn't seem able to. My mother seemed to be considering taking Pam home. She was so distraught, and my father didn't know how to comfort her. He responded by going for a walk, never one to consider "making waves." And never one to tend to anyone else's pain.

These were just the initial hints of Pam's regression, and it was difficult to process, especially since they had been sold a bill of goods that this was where the experts supposedly were. They had assured us that Pam's life would be better there than at home with all of us.

It seemed like Pam went downhill so fast. Her continued regression led to discussions about their initial decision to place her there. I can only imagine, especially as it became more and more obvious that Pam was somehow declining. I know they questioned that decision over and over again.

I felt angry at Mom and Dad for just "accepting" all this. I felt angry that they were so afraid of asking—demanding to know—why Pam seemed to be losing skills. Maybe they did ask. Maybe the real explanation was her seizures or the medications for the seizures or a combination of both. It was just so scary to see someone slipping away as the two people I counted on most weren't able to do anything about it. And I felt angry at God, even though I was not able to fully know why. I thought of singing "Jesus Loves Me" and seeing pictures on the wall of my Sunday School classroom with Jesus holding a young child on his lap. Where was Pammy in this picture?

At the center of it all, it seems to me, was a big lie. My parents had been convinced by strangers that their child needed to be there because she would be cared for by people with more expertise than they had, people who really knew how to care for those with her specific needs. They had been assured that only with the help of these caregivers would Pam's seizures subside. This was not true. There may have been plenty of good, kind, experienced people at that hospital—but they were not experts. And, even as my parents began to feel this in their guts, they hoped they had reason to trust what they had been led to believe.

When it was time to, it was hard to take Pam back to that enormous, white building where she now lived. The mood had changed drastically. I remember feeling sad, having imagined an exuberant family vacation all together. Maybe I had even hoped she would be coming home with us for good. But the reality was that we would be going on to Flintstone Village, and she wouldn't be coming with us.

My gaze shifted back and forth, looking for answers in my parents' faces, but all I saw there was sadness. As we returned to the hospital, the silence and grief hung thick in the air. I racked my brain for the right thing to say or do to put everyone back in the happy, adventurous mood the day had started with. But nothing could be done.

On our way, Pam began waving her arms and vocalizing her little humming song, occasionally grinding her teeth. This was her happy sound I had missed so much. Was she finally comfortable with us again in the unlikely setting of the VW van, enough that she felt safe to sing her song? Was she trying to tell us that her time at the hospital had been a mistake? That it really wasn't the best place for her after all? Did she think we were on our way home? My heart was breaking, and I couldn't keep from crying.

Tears were making their way down my mom's face as we pulled into Custer State Hospital. My dad went around the van and brought Pam's walker to Mom's side, sliding it aside as he reached for Pam. My mom resisted at first, holding onto Pam, but then she let her go. I said goodbye, wondering still if she expected to see us tomorrow. Did she miss us? When I looked into her eyes, I sensed she did and that she didn't understand why we were leaving her there again.

These summer "vacations" continued for many years. The journey seemed less stressful after our younger brother was born in 1967. Martin was able to see Custer State Hospital with a different set of eyes. He had a different experience of growing up with—or without—our sister. His memories of childhood were that he was, in some way, born to take Pam's place and bring purpose to our mother. His visits to Custer weren't defined by being left in that horrible, scary lobby; his big brother and sister were there to reassure him. Even at that dreary place, he was eager to please and would take on the role of pushing Pam around in her chair whenever we went outside.

While Wayne and I had adapted to not asking about where we could go once we were done at the hospital, Martin had no such reservations. His eyes lit up at the mention of Dinosaur Park. He was full of excitement to go climbing on the hills surrounding the state park where we usually camped. Wayne and I enjoyed seeing things through his eyes, setting aside our sadness for a little bit. Even my dad took a short break from chronic sorrow. It was good to hear him laugh and share in the new experience of having Martin around. To all of us, he was a ray of sunshine, and he became my mother's focus.

By the time we visited Custer when I was thirteen or fourteen, Pam could barely hold her head up. She was not able to feed herself, and her happy song occurred less often than ever before. This particular time, we stayed at a motel rather than camping. My mother and I were watching Martin at the pool after having just gotten back from the hospital. I knew from the look on my mother's face what she was thinking about, and feeling brave that day, I brought up the elephant in the room.

"How are you feeling?" I asked her

"Coming to see her never gets easier," my mother explained, "but it isn't as bad as when we first came here. The hardest thing I've ever done was walking out of that room at Custer State Hospital and leaving Pam behind."

"I know that was hard for you. It was hard for me, too, even if I didn't completely understand. Everyone was sad, and I didn't see anything that made me feel like she would be comfortable there."

She seemed surprised by this. "We tried hard to do other things while we were up here—seeing the sites and the tourist attractions. But I'm sure they didn't make up for the real purpose of coming up here, especially for you. I think you feel everything."

I was touched that she recognized my feelings. "How did you manage? After she went to Custer?" I asked her.

My mother was willing to be vulnerable with me in this moment, revealing that if there had ever been a time when she was tempted to numb her pain with substances, coming home without my sister was it. "But I knew I had other responsibilities," she told me. "To you and Wayne, and to your dad, and now Martin."

She went on, "One afternoon, I was in the kitchen getting something ready for supper. Pammy had only been gone for a couple of weeks. All of a sudden, I felt as though my heart skipped a beat. I could physically feel her tugging on the hem of my dress. She used to do that a lot before she left, but I was unprepared to feel that on this day. I couldn't make myself turn and look, afraid of what I might see. Had the whole thing been a bad dream? Was Pammy still here? Or was she trying to tell me she was angry?"

I didn't know what to say. "Mom, she wasn't angry with you. I know that."

She was quiet for a while, steadying herself. "You know, Blackie always used to come to the school because he somehow knew school would be getting out soon."

"Yes, I remember. I don't know how he knew, but he'd be there to 'fetch us' and bring us home," I said.

"When your dad and I were trying to decide what we should do about Custer, Pam started to have crying spells. And the odd thing was that these spells seemed to begin around the time of day you and Wayne were due to come home. I wonder if somehow Pam sensed she was different. Maybe that was why she cried when you were coming home from school."

My mother was almost always good at putting on a brave face around me and Wayne, but as we shared our feelings with each other at the pool, we were both crying. It was devastating to think that Pam may have had to leave our family because she dreaded my return from school, and it was unsettling to hear how painful this experience had been for my mother, who had always seemed disproportionately strong for her four-foot-eleven-and-a-half-inch frame.

As I later reflected on that conversation with my mother, a flashbulb memory added to my devastation: my father, driving a truck on a hot summer day with me in the passenger seat. There was no air conditioning then, and the windows were down. Waiting at the stoplight on Main Street, right in front of the old Redfield Press building, I heard the song "Yesterday" come on the radio. "Why she had to go, I don't know—she wouldn't say. I said something wrong, now I long for yesterday."

It suddenly struck me that maybe I really had said something wrong, and that was why Pam had to go away. Had I hurt her feelings? Asked her questions she didn't understand? I sobbed and sobbed, overwhelmed with self-blame, a response that became second nature to me over time.

Even today, this overwhelming sadness and shame enter my heart for days at a time. I have often asked the families I work with how the brother or sister felt about having a sibling with a disability. Almost always, the parents answer that they thought they were fine, looking at me as if it was an odd question. These families have not necessarily had to experience a child being absent from the family, but even so, the other children often sacrifice a great deal for their sibling—not having friends over as much, having limited activities, having to be prepared for an activity or outing to be canceled, sometimes at the last minute, and a constant expectation to be understanding and willing whenever plans are abruptly changed.

I don't remember anyone ever acknowledging my loss or trying to comfort me. My parents may have assumed I didn't need to be comforted. But I, too, felt the loss of Pamela Sue—

even now, it has never gone away. The loss of her has impacted my life in many ways. Having learned to comfort myself, typically with food, I have been on a diet of some kind for most of my life. Several times, I have had good success when I have worked hard on writing down every morsel I put in my mouth. But I put the weight back on much faster than it came off. Weight has always been a part of my belief that I am not enough, and I believe that the loss of Pam was a big part of this.

We all seem to have experienced this loss differently. I have often tried to share my thoughts about it, especially when other crises arise in our lives. Armed with my psychology books, I would say, "I think this all goes back to Pam." Silence is the standard response, accompanied by a look of bewilderment at my suggestion.

I sensed the looks I received were because it might have sounded like I was blaming her, but I continued trying. I explained that Pam had gone away, and we didn't expect that to happen. Then, we never talked to each other about the loss we had all faced or checked in with each other to see how we were feeling in response to it. On some of those lonely Sunday afternoons, I never once felt that it was okay for me to say, "I miss Pammy today."

When school pictures of me and my brothers were framed and hung on the wall, there were none of Pam. Her pictures stayed in an envelope, somewhere in a drawer or maybe a photo album. We all acted like something so big hadn't happened at all, and that had to be hard on all of us.

No matter what I tried, it seemed as though my family wasn't connecting the same dots that I did. I wasn't blaming her for what happened. *She* was the one who was left behind. But I couldn't seem to find words to communicate what I meant.

Over time, I developed a strategy when asked the question,

"Do you have brothers and sisters?" When talking to some-one who didn't know the back story, I learned to say, "Yes, I have two brothers—one older and one younger," instead of my earlier strategy of "I have two brothers—one older and one younger. And I had a sister. I mean, I still do, but she doesn't live with us. She lives in a special place because she had seizures."

My fumbling was often met with uncomfortably blank stares. I learned it was much easier to protect myself if I also kept our family secret to myself.

I shut my eyes and all the world drops
dead;

I lift my lids and all is born again.

(I think I made you up inside my head.)

~ Sylvia Plath

THE IMPACT
OF LOSS

The Averys never liked to have attention drawn to themselves. No wonder my dad seemed annoyed with me and my brothers, who always seemed to place attention on our family in one way or another—with good behavior or bad. He was afraid of what others would think about us and our antics, which disrupted his attempts to pretend everything was fine. It seems likely that he probably experienced this with his brother, Lloyd, and learned that the best response was to be quiet about it.

Martin knew no boundaries in the area of directing the spotlight to the Avery family. My mom was 36 when he was born. He was unexpected then and has continued to be so throughout his life. Martin brought sunshine and surprise to our family, lifting my parents out of the chronic sorrow, at least temporarily, for many years. He captured our attention and diverted our focus from Pam's absence. With his arrival, a little bit of joy snuck back into our home, and the world moved around him, at least for a while.

Martin's personality delighted most who knew him, which often kept him from experiencing consequences for his actions. Always powered by fun and adventure, he paid little attention to details like making sure he had a pencil and notebook for school. On occasion, he would return from his classes with a piece of masking tape on his shirt that read, "Martin needs a pencil." The teachers soon learned that a note delivered on paper would never make its way to our parents, but if taped to his chest, it would be read. The next day, he would go to school equipped for his lessons.

Martin also experienced the same unpredictable anger from my dad that Wayne and I had. Little episodes like spilling a glass of milk or making a mess were treated as things of major significance. My father's displays of anger, embarrassment, and even shame in reaction to us were something we all carried for a long time.

Starting in fifth grade, I was destined to rock the boat. When I saw that a change needed to be made, I took it upon myself to take care of the problem—and I was all over it. When my dad was still on the police force, a couple of friends and I started to make a plan to replace our town's dog shelter, dissatisfied with its broken-down appearance. So, off we marched to the city police department to make a case for why the city needed a bigger, better dog pound. I was organized in my request, had written down the reasons why these changes should take place, and outlined what my friends and fellow students would do to take care of the dogs and the place that would be built for them to live in. It turns out I had picked the right person to talk to—Bud Kimlicka, the chief of police. Mr. Kimlicka thanked us for coming and said he would hang on to our ideas.

My dad did not bring up the subject of the dog pound,

assuming it was one of my big ideas I wouldn't follow through on. He didn't tell me he was proud of me for having the idea or prouder still that I had brought a complaint to the adult I thought might have some leverage over the issue. As was so often the case, his response was simply to ignore it. There was no conversation on the subject. It was just another thing he seemed embarrassed about. By extension, I felt he was embarrassed of me for bringing my silly ideas to his place of work.

It made me hesitant to involve myself in his work environment again, but there were times when I had to. One summer day, a few of my friends and I were walking home from the swimming pool through the city park when we became aware of someone following us. We recognized the man as someone we knew had talked to young girls and told them he wanted to take pictures of them. At least two of my close friends at the time had experienced this, and seeing the man in the park behind us stirred up an immediate sense of alarm.

Naturally, we were scared and started to run. Moving fast was difficult, wearing thong flip-flops from the pool, and I fell behind the others. Seeing them disappear across the aluminum bridge over Turtle Creek, my sense of terror grew. I felt defenseless, knowing that once we had all crossed that bridge, we'd have a hill to climb before finally reaching the sidewalk that led to the main street of the community. I remember the sound and feel of our feet slapping against the metal bridge as it swayed unsettlingly with our movement. Thankfully, we reached the main street and walked immediately to the police station to file a report on the person we thought had been chasing us. But, despite my fear, my father showed no concern. There was no picking me up to hug me, to say he was glad I was okay and proud that I had known to run and seek help. Instead, there was embarrassment on his face and in his body language. Once again, I was drawing attention to our family. I felt ashamed that he didn't take what had happened seriously.

At that time, people weren't talking much about instances of stalking, grooming, or childhood sexual assault. It was a different time. But we had been followed by a pedophile who was known for talking to children and asking if they would pose for pictures without talking to their parents. What should have been seen as a huge red flag was brushed off as children having wild imaginations. "This man isn't a risk to anyone. He means well," I remember my dad saying. "He's harmless."

The same phrase was used about a relative in our family who had made children uncomfortable by being too close to them, talking about their bodies and appearance, and sometimes even groping them.

And then there was the father of a good friend of mine, who was also a good friend of my dad's. One summer night, during a sleepover, my friend's father came home and sat down to talk with us. Then he pulled us down on his lap and talked about how we were certainly growing up. He felt the breasts of one of my friends, who was developing earlier than the rest of us. Feeling uncomfortable, I called my mom and asked her to come and pick me up. Once I was back home, my father was mostly concerned about why I was home already. "He didn't mean anything by it," he said when I explained, brushing off what I had felt was a threat.

Years later, those comments that minimized the danger of predators remained in my head when I learned a good friend of mine had experienced sexual assault. It seemed easier for my father to simply excuse bad behavior than face the possibility that there may be an ugly truth to people he knew well. As an adult, I continued hearing the same excuses or swift changes of the subject when the topic arose, and the feeling of injustice remained with me, especially once we learned more about what happened to Pamela Sue at Custer State Hospital.

The oldest in my family of origin, Wayne was—and is—steadfast, stoic, dependable, and responsible. However, as a teenager in the 1970s, Wayne refused to get a haircut, which really irked my dad, who wanted his son to look sharp and clean-cut. My father also thought Wayne spent too much time at his girlfriend's house, pointing out that "everyone" noticed and commented on how his car was parked outside her house until late in the evening. He claimed that kind of behavior would lead to higher car insurance premiums, tirades that were typically accompanied by not-so-subtle hints at everything our parents had sacrificed for me and my brother—including my sister—and that they did not appreciate that we continued to act like children.

Other than with his hairstyle, Wayne was not a boat-rocker like Martin and I were as children. But there would come a critical time when his world was shaken to the core at the age of twenty-two. He was graduating from college, had a four-year-old child, and his wife wanted a divorce. His world dropped out from under him in a matter of days. He needed support, and the support that was offered did include a few comforting conversations, but it primarily came in the form of blame and shame. Blame toward my sister-in-law, and shame on Wayne for bringing divorce into the family.

In my mind, I can hear my father's words: "It's a damn shame, that's what it is." I don't even recall if he actually said this about this instance, but such was the pervasive nature of shame in our family. It was the message that rang true in an array of scenarios. And, in this case, the shame was on my big brother. As a result, another opportunity for family support and closeness became something to disregard, not to talk about. We just moved on, much like with the trauma surrounding my sister.

This theme was something I began growing tired of as I was growing up. In junior high, I was tired of everyone expecting certain behaviors from me, and I decided I really wanted to be a badass. A couple of my friends and I huddled in the entryway after lunch, hanging with two brothers, the type of boys who wore long army coats and smoked cigarettes—a clear sign of badassery. I sure thought of myself as walking on the edge—though heaven forbid if anyone got too close to the edge, in which case I was the first to give them a talking to.

In high school, I selected the person I thought was most likely to be trouble. Mark was older than me, and he worked in the lunchroom. From my father, I learned a little about him and knew he didn't have an easy life. Mark's father was a pharmacist at the local drugstore, and his mother had suffered a stroke that took away her ability to really care for herself. He lived with his parents in an apartment upstairs from a local business.

One day, Mark was carrying a load of clothes down to their car, and I saw him drop the basket. He started swearing and looked completely overwhelmed. While this may have been a red flag for most, I saw someone who had a hard life and for whom I could possibly make things better. Once it became official that Mark was my boyfriend, my peer group completely changed. I spent time with Mark and his friends, very rarely seeing the people who used to be my circle of friends. My mother told me my parents were concerned that I was spending too much time with this new peer group. Her approach was softer than my father's would be. When I didn't heed their advice, they confronted me one night when I came home from "riding around" with Mark and his friend, Jim. I responded like a fifteen-year-old, yelling about how they had made home into a living hell. As soon as those words left my mouth, I wanted to take them back.

My father picked up the edge of the kitchen table and slammed it back down. "Don't you tell me about being in hell! Your mother and I went through hell when we took your sister to Custer! You don't know the first thing about what hell is!"

Those words hurt. And I knew my words had hurt him. I went to my room, and neither he nor my mom followed me. It was the only time I saw my father get close to expressing his anger physically.

But I was not going to stop seeing Mark, no matter what they said. I was very drawn to how much I felt he needed rescuing from his life of struggle. He needed guidance, and I felt I was more than equipped to be the person to provide it. After a lifetime of watching everyone's expressions and body language very carefully, listening to things that were said and internalizing them to compare to my own experience, I believed I could provide the support he needed.

Mature beyond my years, I viewed everything from what I considered an adult perspective, not knowing at the time that my adult perspective was not always accurate. I didn't notice when Mark began to exhibit controlling behaviors. I was far from feeling like a child, but I wasn't adult enough to recognize what was happening.

I thought I could share my family with Mark, as imperfect as we were. I wanted to help him feel more secure, to focus on him and his problems, which gave me even more of a reason to separate myself from friends my own age. As I moved away from them, Mark questioned everything I did. He challenged every phone call and every conversation I had with my friends. He showed up at my window in the middle of the night and told me he just couldn't stand being away from me. He would often come in and see me at the local restaurant where I worked. I thought the behavior was kind of romantic—he must really love me. But it only got worse. He started questioning me if he thought I was too talkative to a customer at work. Then, he would stop drinking and being so possessive, and I'd brush off my worries about his less-than-positive characteristics.

Months later, I went into my parents' shop and announced that Mark and I wanted to get married. Maybe this was my chance to keep someone, to stop them from going away. My dad immediately resumed where he had left off with the table incident. He was furious. In an explosive conversation, he told me this relationship wouldn't lead to anything good, and then he left the shop and walked back into the house.

After an hour or two, my mother came home and sat on the arm of the couch, talking to me about what I had said. Getting married was not necessarily out of the question, she said. She told me they would talk more about it but not to count on anything changing. My father talked to our pastor at the United Methodist Church and was given examples of other young marriages that had made it work. Eventually, they gave their permission. I was sixteen.

When I was leaving to pick up the dress I had ordered through the local JCPenney store, Mark stopped me before I got in the car. We got into an argument about where I had been, and I went home in tears. As much as I wanted to tell my mom what was going on, the only thing I managed to get out was that he was really jealous. I didn't tell her about the times he would show up at my bedroom window or place of work to tell me he needed me. At sixteen, none of that sounded like someone who would tear me down and stop me from being who I was. It sounded like a fairy tale that only encouraged me to stay the course.

Years later, when I asked my parents why they gave me their permission and told them I wished I could turn back time, my mother said they figured it would be better to let me get married then rather than trying to keep us apart, where I then might be more likely to get pregnant in order to force the decision, which would only bring more shame to the family. They may also have felt desperate not to lose another daughter.

And then there was Martin, always a leader and always surrounded by friends. He was smart, creative, and often expected to carry something out with absolutely no guidance. Many times, he was put in a position to complete something that was far beyond his years and capabilities, especially by our father. When he couldn't do whatever it was, he was shamed and made to feel like he had failed.

As a high school sophomore on a band trip, Martin and a few of his friends ventured away from the hotel, visited a bar, and returned to the hotel with alcohol, which they hid in the ceiling of their room. Somehow, among this group of teenagers, word got out, and they were caught. As a result, he was suspended from school for three days and kicked out of band for the remainder of the school year.

My father was very angry and responded as usual, which resulted in Martin admitting that he had been drinking for a long time—to the point of passing out—since he was eleven years old. My father's reply was to emit a long sigh, peering at Martin over the top of his glasses as he slid one hand back and forth over the other, as he often did when he was doing some serious thinking.

"You sure picked a fine time to hit us with this," he said in covert reference to the latest news about Pam, which none of us dared speak of aloud. Then, my father got up, left the kitchen, and went outside. It was a pattern we were all so familiar with: say the hurtful thing, end the conversation, and go out the door, leaving my mother to handle the clean-up. "He didn't mean it," "I'll talk to him," and, ultimately, "You need to go apologize to your dad." Our father was always the avoider, and Mother was always the fixer, the go-between, the one we each went to when we couldn't figure out our dad. If there were little things to which we confessed, she smoothed it over with him. But her fixing didn't always work.

Upon his disclosure, no help was offered to my brother. No efforts were made to determine the seriousness of his early drinking, the reasons why it was happening, or how he might have been supplied with the alcohol. He was not offered counseling or even further discussion. He was treated as the problem.

In my heart, I knew the reason behind this behavior was our family. I thought about how much Martin looked up to Mark and how Mark regarded my family as odd because we never had alcohol at our house or as part of our celebrations. And, of course, I thought about Pam, who had left us in a state of brokenness that began many years prior. On his own, Martin decided that he was an alcoholic and quit drinking altogether. He began traveling with his own six-pack of Tab soda and managed to become an ultimate concert-goer without alcohol ever being involved. I was proud of him.

Meanwhile, as my parents were struggling to handle their at-home children in our struggles of growing up, communication about my sister became irregular at best. My parents were hungry to hear anything from those caring for Pamela at Custer State Hospital. They wanted to hear about her progress, her everyday activities, her health condition and seizures, and stories of her developing traits and skills. Marilyn had been the one person there who cared for Pam, frequently contacting my parents to share information about her life, assuring them that she was still a person with her own mischievous personality who would go into the nurse's office with her walker and pull papers and things off the desk. She told them she, too, knew Pam's happy sound. This meant so much.

They always looked forward to these little conversations, but before long, Marilyn stopped contacting them. Curious about the reason, they later asked and were informed that she had been told by her supervisors it was not appropriate for her to be communicating with the family this way. My parents couldn't comprehend this. Why should a family be completely cut off from knowing anything about their child? About their day, their well-being, their personality—the things that matter most to loved ones.

Having now spent a number of years in agency and school administration, I have an idea why this happened. Sometimes, when a staff person develops a close personal relationship with a family and has conversations with them about their child, they may have a different perspective regarding how to manage the child's care. Sometimes, their perspective may not even be accurate. As a result, the parent is often encouraged to direct all questions about a care program to a teacher or administrator. This may be efficient and reassuring to staff, but it has the potential to do significant damage to relationships, all for the sake of consistent, accurate information.

There can be good reasons for having some control over the flow of information. However, it can also increase parents' concern about what may or may not be happening to their child. In our case, those deemed "appropriate" communicators lacked any first-hand knowledge of what a day in the life of my sister was actually like. They didn't know that she was mischievous, whether she was purposeful in communicating her wants and needs, or if she was experiencing anything her parents ought to have been informed of. Systems, even those with good intentions, may have a devastating effect on communication and relationships.

The realization that those in power typically want to keep all information coming from one place formed my deep belief in transparency. That belief is built into how I approach special education, dictated by the law and the essence of the law—that parents and educators are partners in developing the "contract" that holds us to carry out the goals we agreed upon. When we lost the stories of Pam wheeling into the nurse's office and cleaning off the desktop and of the days when she seemed particularly happy, we lost my sister all over again.

Doubt is a pain
  Too lonely to know

  That faith

Is his twin brother

- Kahlil Gibran

SOMETHING
TO PROVE

I was a very good student, maintaining a solid GPA and on track to graduate in 1976. All things I didn't need to be an athlete to excel in, I did—band, debate, and declam. My main peer group was made up of people four to five years older than me and already part of the workforce, and high school seemed less and less important. Academically, I was never concerned I wouldn't graduate, and I needed a job, so I went to my principal and asked about changing my schedule in order to work for part of the day while attending my classes the other part.

The timing of my request was not good, the principal explained. Two other couples in high school had been granted such permission, but they were expecting a child. When I asked why their situation was so different from mine, I wasn't given an answer. The principal simply explained that he felt he had been getting too many of these requests all at one time, and he didn't want to discuss it further.

Without consulting my teachers or checking my transcripts at all, he kept our conversation brief and posed a decisive question: Did I want to continue my classes and finish high school or quit school and get married? All I had been asking for was a flexible schedule, but when he laid it out so starkly, the choice was reframed entirely.

At that point, I was afraid to turn the ship around. So I went to my locker, gathered my books, turned them in to the office, and quit high school. No one approached my parents or asked them questions about the changes I had displayed over the course of that year, even though they were now resulting in such an uncharacteristic outcome. No one scheduled a meeting with all concerned to determine if a plan could be made to help me succeed. No one asked me questions or encouraged me to stay in school.

By the time my wedding day approached, my parents were aware that there were problems in my relationship—that my husband-to-be was jealous and controlling. I guess they thought, as I did at the time, that marrying him would somehow solve those issues.

So, on November 4, 1974, three months away from seventeen, I put on a navy blue polyester pantsuit and packed my suitcase for the trip to Wall, South Dakota, to get married. As I waited outside with my parents, I momentarily hoped they would ask me if I was sure I wanted to go through with this, that they would say I didn't have to. That they would ask me what they hadn't been able to ask Pam: to stay home.

When Mark drove up, I told myself we would be okay. Even though the relationship was not a healthy one, I believed with all my heart that we were meant to be together. As we drove to Wall, though, I felt all of the loneliness and abandonment that were with me throughout my childhood.

On our special day, Mark was not in the best mood. When I went in to change and get ready for the ceremony, he was irritated and wanted to know how long it would take. Unlike in the movies, where others happily assist the bride as she gets ready, it was just me, walking on eggshells and hurrying through the process to be sure he wouldn't be angry.

I was happy to see Reverend Morrison at the Methodist Church, where we would be saying our vows. He had been the minister from our church, whom I had gotten to know quite well when I went through confirmation class. In response to the many challenging questions I posed about the Bible and whether everything in it was, in fact, from God, he would look at me and say, "I can always count on you to ask the $64,000 questions." It was a comfort to have him and his wife there for my support, but it was nothing like having my mom and my dear friends with me on my wedding day.

Reverend Morrison did what he could to make our ceremony feel special, and his wife made sure to at least take a picture of us, but it was more awkward than anything else. When it was over, we drove to Rapid City and checked into a budget motel. There was no joy on this day, but I was somewhat accustomed to not feeling joyful.

After the "honeymoon," we returned to Redfield and my job at the coffee shop. Eventually, I ended up getting my GED, and Mark and I rented a small house near my parents for eighty-five dollars a month. It was a nice house, and we were going to live happily ever after.

Mark quickly learned how to reupholster furniture from my mother, who had her own side of my parents' shop, which was draped with huge rolls of upholstery fabric hanging on display for customers. Our furniture was refurbished and reupholstered and, therefore, different from most of the furniture we had seen in stores. Meanwhile, I created macramé plant hangers to place in various spots and found the perfect spot for the precious cedar chest that had been my mother's and for my guitar poster with the words "Peace to All Who Enter Here." Our home was coming together, and things seemed to be looking up for us.

My hours working at the coffee shop varied. Sometimes, I would get a call early in the morning from my boss asking if I could come in early because another worker didn't show up. Other times, they were having a slow day, and my boss would tell me to go home. Mark was uncomfortable each time a sudden scheduling change took place. He was suspicious about why my boss called, wondering who had *really* called and where I was actually going. I was berated with questions like, "How is it you were the one who happened to get off early? What's the story there?" These questions always caught me off guard. I couldn't imagine they were serious—but they were.

Living with Mark was exhausting. I never left the house feeling like I wouldn't have to explain myself. If I came home from the grocery store, he would demand to see the receipt and insinuate that I had written a check for more and kept the difference. If I was driving, I found myself checking my surroundings. If I ended up on a street that was out of the expected route, I began to panic, worrying that if something happened—if I had an accident or my car broke down—I would have to explain where I was and why I was there. And, driving in the car with Mark, if a male driver gave the "South Dakota wave," lifting his index finger off the steering wheel, it must be because I had been with him. I felt trapped, like I was living with someone who didn't know me at all. And I was.

Mark's mother came to spend a few days with us. Feeling totally left out of their conversation, I went to bed, but I could hear them discussing my behavior and suspicious schedule. His mother didn't challenge him or stick up for me. I lay in bed, feeling like I was listening to two people who were supposed to love me but were describing someone I didn't even recognize. As the tears rolled down my face, I remember wanting nothing more than to get dressed, go downstairs, and walk the half block down to my parents' home. At seventeen years old, I just wanted to go home. I felt like I had never been so alone before.

And then it dawned on me—of *course* I had. I had felt this way plenty of times since Pam left, where all I wanted was to return to the home life I knew. I remembered missing her so much, but I didn't let on or let my parents hear me crying. I don't know what would have happened if I had acted on this longing I felt, if I had actually left our new house and gone "home." I suspect I would have been encouraged to work it out, reminded that I had made my bed and needed to lie in it until I figured things out for myself. I felt there was no escaping it, and it was a "damn shame." So much so that the shame overwhelmed me.

From seventeen to eighteen, I moved around jobs a bit. Thinking it would improve our situation, I took a full-time job at a local grocery store, which promised a consistent schedule, and quickly learned that no longer being called in early didn't make much of a difference in the way I was treated. While many of my former classmates were heading off to college, I surprised myself by considering a job at Redfield State Hospital and School, where several of my classmates were working while deciding what they were going to do with their lives.

I had never imagined working there, at a place like that, but something about it felt promising with the consistent hours and pay. When I was considering taking the job, I thought of it as a kind of retribution for the fact that I hadn't stood up for Pam when she was growing up in an institution similar to this one.

At the same time, it seemed like a betrayal of some sort, the thought of giving care and attention to these patients when my own sister had been clear across the state for years, so far from her family's care.

I was still angry with God and argumentative with others, believing that "a loving God" would not have taken so much away from my sister or left a big hole in our family that could never be filled. Resistant to spending every day in a place that constantly reminded me of my family's fraught situation, I was initially adamant about not working at Redfield. Nonetheless, I sensed there was an opportunity for personal growth there, and I began working as a houseparent, providing direct care to residents at the age of eighteen.

I learned a great deal working as a newly hired staff member at RSHS. In my opinion, the job was more than equivalent to a college degree, and it offered benefits and a higher wage than being a cashier at Ken's Super Valu, as well as more responsibility. I was tasked with direct care, which involved feeding and bathing patients, accompanying them to the bathroom, monitoring and reporting any illnesses to the nurse as she made rounds, and keeping everyone in the unit safe. Working there collided with all my memories of my sister—all the heartache and the resentment I had about her being at Custer. I thought about her every single day and saw her in so many others around me. To cope, I set a goal for myself: to keep thinking of her and do my best to be for my patients the kind of person I hoped was there with her.

I was assigned to work the 7-to-3 shift between two buildings, Elmview and Clark. Those of us who worked between different buildings like that had to call in to the switchboard operator every day to find out where we had to go that day. Clients on Elmview, especially its first floor, were the most significantly disabled females. It was not a welcoming place. The dorm was locked, and those of us who were not yet assigned a permanent position did not have keys. The entryway was cold, resembling the marble lobby area at Custer.

Once inside, the huge dayroom was no cozier or more welcoming. The wide-open space sported marble floors, and immensely high ceilings were like nothing I had expected. Large green rocking chairs lined the walls, ready for residents to sit in—that's how the women who lived there in 1976 were referred to—though many of them preferred to pace around on foot or sit directly on the floor. Also at the ready were an array of mop buckets, as the marble floors lent themselves to regular bathroom incidents. Despite the efforts made by the "houseparents" or "resident workers," bathroom visits weren't always successful, and the water in the mop buckets had to be changed constantly to keep the smell under control.

Windows let in lots of light along the west side of the building; they didn't appear to open, but they nearly reached the top of the very high ceiling. Food was delivered on individual trays to the dining room, adjacent to the dayroom, through a system of underground tunnels that were operational under the entire institution. Some of the residents could feed themselves, but most could not.

People back then made a distinction between residents and individuals, in that, this place was thought of as a patient's home. It was an indication of progress slowly being made toward person-first thinking. The philosophies behind disability care were gradually evolving, and there was hope for improvement. Intentional terminology applied also to those of us who worked there. Resident workers were residents who were higher functioning and were therefore assigned units to work in, responsible for keeping the facilities clean as well as providing direct care services to less functional residents who needed the assistance.

The dormitory area was filled with single beds topped with red cloth bedspreads. Stripping off the wet bedding and remaking the beds came with a small bit of satisfaction because it was one of few operations that seemed to have a sense of order to it. All dirty sheets were removed and bagged to send off to the laundry, and then the beds were remade with care, ensuring the curved bottom of the sheet was correctly matched to the lower end of the mattress. I took comfort in this process, imagining that I was contributing to bedtime being a safe space. When the beds were all freshly made with clean linens, the room almost appeared like a normal place for over twenty adults to share.

Getting everyone dressed and ready for the day was interesting, as most residents wore clothing an outsider would view as quite abnormal. Some wore one-piece jumpsuits, while others dressed in canvas "outfits" that looked very much like straitjackets. Some wore these over their clothes; for others, it was their entire ensemble.

These canvas numbers were multi-purpose. They were tied in such a way that they were difficult to remove, as many of the women did not keep clothing on. They were also used as restraints when residents needed assistance to use the bathroom, the canvas ties securing to the arms of the portable commodes so the residents would remain on the toilet until someone decided they had been there long enough.

This was something I did not expect. In my eyes and my heart, it was inhumane. It reminded me of the canvas mittens Pam wore, which we were told were tied securely to correct certain behaviors of hers, including her form of sensory stimulation—chewing on her hands. For many individuals, these types of restraints were used to prevent them from touching themselves for stimulation and sometimes from picking up objects that may be dangerous. The practice, including physical holds of children, has been under scrutiny for years. Once again, change has taken place in small steps for a variety of programs, though the American Medical Association (AMA) now recommends use of the least restrictive restraint possible for each situation, paired with frequent patient assessment.

In lieu of factual background information, veteran houseparents delighted in crafting folklore on many of the individuals in their care. Their stories included the legend behind the woman who insisted on taking off her clothes, which involved her being brought to the state school in the back of an old pickup truck. Reportedly, she weighed over five hundred pounds. She had lost hundreds of pounds since her admission, and her skin now sagged around her bones. Some speculated she had never been dressed at all before coming there.

There was another woman who, depending on the storyteller, was either possessed by demons or was insane as well as mentally retarded. Many individuals, in fact, were dual diagnosed, and this woman's story was told to scare the shit out of newcomer employees to the dorm. "Be watchful," they'd be warned. "She gets upset when there are different people here. She can always tell if there are more houseparents here than there are supposed to be. She knows there are always three or four. Any more than that, and she'll start something." Whatever it meant, the tale was enough to scare those of us who were new to the environment.

While these stories may not have been based on fact, they may have had some accuracy about them. People could be institutionalized for more reasons than merely needing specialized care. It wasn't unheard of for a mother of several children to be institutionalized, not due to mental illness or disability but to poverty, sometimes leaving behind a father who couldn't care for the children by himself. Or a husband may have decided that his wife was being promiscuous, in which case institutionalization could be an option.

These were among the many interesting and often upsetting details I learned before I eventually moved into a regular position and was permanently assigned to Clark, no longer having to float between two buildings. Working there changed my perspective completely. Clark was a one-story building with four wings, and the atmosphere was more like a nursing home. I worked mostly on Clark South, the wing devoted to caring not for the elderly like the other three but mostly for children. It was clean and comfortable and bright, and the staff were kind, for the most part. Still, much of the custodial work was completed by resident workers, but at least the staff of Clark Building were kind to them and not interested in humiliating each other or the residents.

The women I typically worked with on Clark South were all much older than I—some by a few years, others by decades. Arlene was the mama bear of all of us, including the residents. She was a large woman, and she was always hot, so, no matter the temperature, she wore a sleeveless top and shorts. She did not have an easy home life and likely felt more valued at work than at home. I imagine she may have felt that work was a place where she could exercise greater control over her surroundings, and she did that by being good to everyone around her. The same was probably true for me, even if I didn't realize it at the time. I can still see her sitting at the head of the table in her shorts and sleeveless top, smoking a cigarette, which was still permitted inside the facility at that time. I was relieved to find that the tone and the treatment of the residents here were so very different from the darkness at the other building. It felt more like a family, and I prayed that my sister had someone to care for her like these women cared for our residents and me.

Christopher and Michelle were two of the younger ones on Clark South. Both of them had microcephaly, characterized by cognitive disabilities and a very small head, and their brains did not develop properly. They both wore leg braces that seemed very similar to the ones that Pamela Sue wore. It was interesting to learn more about the braces and the course of treatment from the physical therapy staff, who were phenomenal there.

One of the children on Clark South often had severe grand mal seizures. It was easy to tell when she was going into one, as she very definitely experienced an aura, a phenomenon that some people experience before a seizure. It can involve abnormal sensations such as changes in vision, hearing, taste, or smell; feelings of déjà vu, panic, or detachment; and the sound of voices or buzzing. This child would begin to cry, biting her hand and moving in circles before the onset of a seizure. Once it took its full effect, we would often have to call the infirmary for an injection that would bring her out of it. These seizures lasted a long time, and our nursing staff talked about the importance of calling immediately whenever this little girl had a seizure. Those of us who could be calm, myself included, started the vigil and remained with her as her body strained and moved at will, waiting for the nurse or doctor to arrive.

I had observed seizures before, and although it was scary to watch this child, I stayed by her side and helped as the staff arrived to assist us. I remember the feeling of frustration and heartbreak when we had to wait longer because no doctor was on staff, which meant she seized much longer than necessary. In some ways, it took me back to the time when my family's life was turned upside down, waiting for a doctor to arrive. But I could be calm and rational, focusing instead on responding in a way that was appropriate for someone with my level of responsibility.

I moved quickly through the training process of becoming a houseparent II and then a houseparent III, which meant more and more responsibility in supervising others. Maxine Minnick, Clark's unit director, was a tall woman who always carried herself with poise and grace and dressed professionally. She was not a very confrontational person—unless she had to be—but she was a leader like no other.

When staff lingered too long over coffee, Ms. Minnick would say, "Good morning," glancing over her shoulder at the clock as she walked directly to the dorm to begin interacting with the residents. Without a word, we were reprimanded, and we knew it. It was her way of displaying leadership while allowing us to save face, not directly telling us to get where we needed to be, and it was what we all admired about her.

Every single one of us would do anything for her, which ultimately resulted in better care of the residents. I learned a lot about leadership from her, and she was among the heroes who inspired me and whom I hope I emulated when I became an administrator in my thirties. As I continued to progress in my career, I have thought of her often, wanting those I supervised to describe me as someone who did not need power over others but someone who allows others grace rather than pursuing direct confrontation.

I have seen many examples of people in power being nasty and doing so because they have no power over their own lives and, therefore, seek power over others. This type of power is most often built on force, coercion, domination, and control and is motivated largely by fear. By contrast, power *with* is a shared power that grows out of collaboration and relationships. It is built on respect, mutual support, shared responsibility, solidarity, influence, empowerment, and collaboration. In this environment, we were all able to grow more accustomed to doing things our own way and with more consideration for the residents, less concerned about appeasing leaders who govern from a "power over" mindset.

There was an institution-wide practice for houseparents to take a couple of residents with them to the canteen to purchase treats for the dorm. One day, Connie, another houseparent near my age with whom I had developed a great relationship, suggested, "What about Annie? She could go," referring to an elderly and often grumpy resident who could almost fit a description of someone who is homeless, always dressed in many layers with a large CPO jacket on top. This brought a laugh from Lucille and the others.

With unexpected delight, our coworkers said we could be the ones to bring her. What they didn't tell us was that Annie also picked up items, stuffing them in her pockets or her bra or wherever she could find space. Turns out she was a bit of a hoarder as well as a thief. So when Connie, Annie, and I arrived back at the dorm with our treats, they then searched Annie, emptying the contents of all she had stolen. The activity was designed to teach us why it wasn't worth changing up the way things worked on this unit. Lesson learned, but it didn't stop us from finding other ways to interact and engage with the residents, always striving to be kind and compassionate to them instead of ignoring them—or, worse, making fun of them.

Sometimes, the ways we thought of including the residents in activities weren't entirely thought through. During Christmastime, I came up with an idea I felt good about, but I didn't think of how my actions would be perceived by others. I decided to take one of the children with me to my parents' house for Christmas dinner and selected Christopher, a child on the unit with microcephaly. I knew he had been left when he was born and had no family to visit him or make sure his Christmas was happy. Excited, I went through the paperwork to get permission for this, planning for whatever things he may need, even though he would only be visiting one afternoon.

When Christopher arrived on Christmas Day, my family was not nearly as jubilant as I was. They were kind and asked a few questions about his disability, but my father and Wayne were visibly unhappy. My dad spent time out in the garage, and Wayne seemed bewildered by what had been going through my head, bringing this child to our home when our own family member in a similar condition was far away, alone and without us on Christmas.

I could understand Wayne's feelings, but I had hoped for a different outcome. I suppose I was hoping for some way of reaching out to and providing a different experience for this little boy I took care of day to day. By bringing Christopher home on this day, I wanted to help my family see something in him, to recognize that our relationship could help him enjoy the holiday even when a family of his own could not.

I was also hoping to discover that maybe we were all finally ready to talk about our own experience—that seeing this child in a positive light would, at last, generate the conversation and familial support we had been avoiding for so long. That maybe we would finally laugh on this holiday rather than feel bogged down by the inescapable sadness of it. But that would mean breaking one of our family's unspoken rules. This rule was that we had to be careful not to have "too much fun." As long as Pam was not with us, we had to keep the fun to a minimum. If we didn't, we should probably settle down so as not to make ourselves sick.

I have given you authority to trample on
snakes and scorpions and to overcome
all the power of the enemy; nothing will
harm you.

~ Luke 10:19

SHE CAN'T
STAY THERE

As a nineteen-year-old, I went to see Pam by myself. It had been a few years since I had visited Custer, but I had been working at the Redfield State Hospital and School for a year now, and my many experiences there had led me to wonder more about the care that Pam was receiving. After years of questions that were met with less and less insight into her daily life and progress, I was ready for answers.

Mark reluctantly agreed to go with me, though he would not come into the building, and we got in the car for the long drive. On the way to Custer, I thought about my experiences up until this time. I knew by now that resident workers were not always treated well by houseparents, that they were often directed to do the cleaning jobs those in power did not want to touch themselves and belittled if they didn't do so to their standards. Sometimes, they were even punished if they argued or refused the task. And then I thought about Edith.

Edith was a large, very strong woman with dark hair that was cut in a straight line just above her eyebrows. She had a kind of Neanderthal look and dressed in a large shift dress of sorts. She was nearly non-verbal and walked around with a baby doll in her arms. Some of the staff seemed to enjoy teasing her by taking the baby doll away from her, especially when she demonstrated behavior they considered problematic.

Taking the baby doll away typically made Edith cry and scream and sometimes twist her body around in protest. It was funny to some of the staff if it brought on an epileptic seizure, and they speculated whether the seizure was real or fake.

I was still the new kid working on the unit when I first saw how she was treated, and yet I was appalled by it, frozen. Not wanting to rock the boat, I did the only thing I knew to do at this time: fume inside, think about reporting it to the supervisors, and then ultimately decide against it. I was too new at the job, and if I kept the job, I knew it would make the staff—and therefore the work itself—more difficult. Oddly, the same people who teased Edith in this way frequently also seemed to demonstrate real affection for her at other times. And I found myself feeling confused about that.

This pattern with Edith was later played out as a means of demonstrating to new program staff what was what. One of the concepts being introduced was that of age-appropriateness, wherein adults were discouraged from playing with children's toys and encouraged to interact with something more "appropriate." There is some logic to this philosophy, but it disregards that some individuals had always played with toys traditionally meant for children, and the transition to other items was not always successful. Such was the case when a case manager came to the dorm, brought Edith out, removed her baby doll from her arms, and let the screams begin. To this day, I have zero tolerance for teasing.

I wondered if Pam was experiencing any of the kind of treatment I had witnessed at Redfield, and I was finally ready to dig deeper. As a child visiting Custer, I had not been allowed to visit the actual residents' ward, so my memories were practically non-existent. In my mind, though, I pictured it as a series of private rooms off of a hallway, more of a hospital-like setting than what I observed at RSHS. Knowing Custer had operated as a TB sanatorium before 1963, I knew better than to expect large dormitory rooms or many luxuries, but I hoped Pam and the other residents were nonetheless receiving the care and comfort they needed and deserved.

My thoughts stopped racing once I looked up and saw the familiar CUSTER sign on the mountain. It was a rainy Saturday afternoon, and I was showing up unannounced. I walked into the building alone and was escorted down the hallway to the residents' quarters. I soon found Pam hunched over in the middle of the floor. She was alone, her hands covered in the big canvas mitten restraints they often kept on her. Her hair was greasy and uncombed, and she didn't appear to be cared for in the way I would have expected. She seemed groggy and out of it. My first impression didn't do much to assuage my worries, but I tried not to show my concern, not wishing to cause my sister distress.

After a few minutes, Pam's caretaker suggested I might want to leave because it was time for her to eat. I said I would stay and that I could feed her. The caretaker agreed, bringing Pam's tray to me. I took it from her and noticed all the food was pureed. When I asked why that was the case, she said that Pam was given a special-order diet to prevent choking, and then she showed me how to pour the nasty liquid so that Pam would swallow it.

It was a dehumanizing scene, and, in my gut, I knew something was wrong. I couldn't imagine Pam being fed like this day after day, like an abandoned baby bird, with no sense of agency or dignity. How could an individual be expected to progress in these conditions? It was like they had given up on her.

I was distraught, but one wants to trust those who are considered experts at what they have been appointed to do. So, I didn't say anything to anyone about how disappointed I was in the lack of care she was evidently experiencing. The drive home was long, and all I wanted was to talk to my parents about what I had seen. As soon as I got back, I went to their house, visibly upset.

"I went to visit Pam," I told them, already shaking. "It didn't go well."

They were immediately on edge by my raised voice.

"What do you mean by that?" my mother asked. "Was she sick?"

"No, but she was a mess," I explained. "I didn't tell them I was coming in advance because I wanted to see what it's actually like there. She was in a room all alone with those horrible canvas mittens on. Just sitting there with nothing to do and no one watching her." Recalling the scene, I was infuriated all over again. "You wouldn't believe how dirty she was. Her hair hadn't been washed for days—maybe weeks!"

They didn't like what I was saying, but they didn't tell me to stop as I continued to explain what I had seen and the terrible feeling I had.

"We have to get her out of there," I concluded finally.

As soon as I heard the words "settle down," a common plea in the Avery household, I started to cry.

"Don't cry," my mother said. "You'll make yourself sick."

It's exactly what I had been told my entire life. For over a decade now, I had always been encouraged not to display my big emotions. When I was little, the resistance to my emotional displays frightened me. I had wondered why crying was always treated as some kind of threat. What would happen to me if I just cried? Would I be like Pam? Now, I knew better, and I had had enough.

"I will *not* get sick if I cry! What is wrong with you?" I demanded.

They both stood there in silent shock, not knowing what to say next.

"I'm trying to tell you something important. It is horrible there! Don't you believe me? Don't you want her out of a horrible place? The thought of her staying—*that* is what makes me sick!"

My mother made some comment about how they were likely just short-staffed on the weekends before continuing to stand there mutely as my father exited the room. Tears streaming down my face, it was clear to me that my parents had no intention of further investigating or complaining about Pam's care. Angrier than ever, I left the house, slamming the screen door behind me.

With the images of Pam in my mind, I knew that I would change the situation if I could. If I hadn't been just a child when she was sent away, I would have been a better advocate for Pam. I would have gone to see her more often and been more involved in her treatment and the important decisions made for her.

I couldn't do more then, but I would now. I made a commitment then and there to do whatever I could for her and others. I would stand up and make noise.

Everyone and everything around you is your teacher.

~ Ken Keyes Jr.

A DIFFERENT PATH

As I continued to be invested in my work of helping others, it became clear that despite my painstaking efforts, my marriage wasn't working. Two years in, Mark was clearly not interested in improving upon our situation. Yet leaving the marriage would mean that I had failed at the important commitment I had made to becoming my husband's family, solving all of his insecurities, and sharing my family with him. As I tried to stay positive over the years, he only became more and more angry, drinking more and continuing to be jealous, possessive, and outright miserable. He was intent on making me miserable in kind, and it was working.

Two years after I started at RSHS, I applied for a position as an occupational therapy aide, which really meant arts and crafts aide. Laurie, the other aide, and I did a variety of crafts and leisure activities with the residents each day. This was a relatively new position, brought about by the idea that individuals with intellectual disabilities couldn't just sit passively in their dorm for hours on end without stimulation or enjoyment of any kind. Another indication that times were gradually changing, it presented an opportunity to learn different things.

The talk at this time was all about "programming." New staff were hired as case managers, whose job was to separate the residents into groups and identify needs to address through simple behavior management programs. This included teaching primarily self-help skills, such as dressing independently, toileting, tooth brushing, and feeding. Some of the people who had worked there for a long time were skeptical, at times arrogantly so, about whether anyone could change residents' skills and behavior. Some did their best to sabotage the success of this new way of approaching care.

I, on the other hand, was pleased about and open to these developments, and before long, I saw how individuals were, in fact, making progress. My motivation to embrace these new ideas wholeheartedly came from the hope that such opportunities were also being afforded to my sister over at Custer.

Working in the basement classroom area with Laurie, it was gratifying to see what the residents could do when given the chance. We stayed busy with finding projects for the adult residents to work on and accomplish and were able to purchase plenty of supplies. It was one of my first experiences in a classroom-like setting, and I was inspired about where the program might lead. This job was also less stressful and physically challenging for me while I was pregnant.

In February of 1979, my daughter of light, Amber Lynn, was born. The stars were in alignment as she entered the world on the twenty-fifth of the month, right between my mother's birthday on the twenty-third and mine on the twenty-seventh—strong Pisces women.

While on maternity leave, I could not imagine returning to

work, so I resigned and started an in-home daycare. It was fun but exhausting, with early mornings and late nights. I savored every minute of being home with my own baby, but after a couple years, all the time with her had me thinking hard about what I wanted for my life. Eventually, the seeds I was planting were nurtured into a decision: I wanted to go back to school, get my degree as a speech therapist, and advance my career.

When I mentioned the idea of going back to school, Mark was livid. He laughed at the thought and said I would never be able to do it, when what he was most afraid of was that I could. The argument went on for weeks. It was brought up to my parents, who were also discouraging—not because they doubted my abilities but because they didn't believe it made sense to borrow money to go to school. What could I do with a degree, anyway, but be a pencil pusher at the state school? And to be in debt for that? They also reminded me that my daughter would have to be put in daycare, which would be another major expense.

In spite of my husband's response, I began researching Northern State College in Aberdeen as well as student loans and grants I could apply for. I had an interesting talk with someone at the bank, who explained that they "just didn't give loans to freshman students." In return, I asked him, "Then how does one become a sophomore?" Upon further inquiry, I discovered that I was eligible for a Pell Grant and wouldn't have to borrow as much money as I thought. I talked to my pastor, too, who only said, "Sometimes we have to step out on faith."

So that's exactly what I did. In the spring of 1981, without my husband's blessing, I enrolled in classes at Northern State College. My NSC transcripts would include a notation at the top of the first page: "Entered on probation with GED."

A good friend of mine who had her own home daycare

agreed to care for Amber, and I arranged to carpool with other people who lived in Redfield and drove to NSC in Aberdeen. The fact that I managed to get this far gave me hope that things could work out. One thing I knew was that I was going to finish college—maybe a little at a time, but I would finish. But Mark's jealousy and controlling behavior only escalated further.

We continued to fight and argue about my going to school. I was on the dean's list that semester and most of the semesters that followed, and I loved what I was learning and being around other people every day. My confidence was growing, and Mark believed I would leave him once I was done with school, which only escalated our growing tension.

Unfortunately, the efforts to sabotage my educational dreams were again successful. Perhaps because misery loves company, paired with a financial aid glitch, I reluctantly withdrew from school and went back to work at RSHS. I felt betrayed by my husband as well as my parents, who—in my adulthood as in my childhood—couldn't see me, what I needed, or what I was capable of accomplishing.

While it felt like a personal sacrifice, going back to work at RSHS turned out to be enjoyable and comfortable. I continued to learn all that I could, still hopeful that one day I would go back and finish my degree. I was assigned to Cottage Two, whose floor plan was similar to the Clark building but with newly built units. Instead of the huge dayroom, the units had normal living rooms and bedrooms shared only by a couple of individuals. I worked with a group of younger boys, a couple of whom I knew from the Clark building. Once again, I was grateful to work with good people and form good relationships— including my friend, Connie.

One day, Connie and I were struck with another one of our ideas. We wanted to paint one of the walls in the small dayroom, imagining how it would brighten up the area and hoping it could become a place for visitors to sit comfortably with their loved ones, which I had sorely lacked as a child sitting in the lobby of Custer State Hospital.

We had envisioned a beautiful rainbow; however, when we talked to the paint shop about our ideas, we discovered that RSHS only purchased neutral colors. So, we proposed a different plan and asked if they could somehow add color to white. Our unit director was on board and signed off on our requisition for the project, reminding us that it was a big undertaking and that we would need to complete it on our own time. We agreed and got to work sketching out the rainbow and then beginning to paint. Connie and I worked hard, and at the end, we stood back and proudly admired our completed project. The last time I ran into one of the staff who remains on Cottage Two , she told me that our rainbow still adorns the wall there.

Even with the chaos at home and the disappointment of quitting school once again, I had to admit I was thriving at work. I found all of the residents interesting, each with their own personalities that were so intriguing to me, just as Pam's unique personality traits and forms of expression had charmed me so as a child.

The other staff members also seemed to see something in me, and they provided encouragement in my work with the residents. One of the boys on Cottage Two was Brian, a gentle boy who I would speculate was somewhere on the autism spectrum. He was non-verbal and walked about the Cottage, sliding one palm over the other in a rhythmic way. He seemed content, and he seemed to gravitate toward me within a short time together.

With time, I moved into the role of psychiatric technician (psych tech), which came with the responsibilities of a trainer, carrying out programs to teach residents the various skills they would need to learn to do independently. This was my wheel-house. I believed that these children could learn, and I clearly understood the goal and the teaching strategies needed for them to make progress.

I had a small space within a room that was used as an office, and I often heard Brian wandering in, recognizable by the distinctive scuffle of his feet and the noise he made when he was sliding his palms together. It was like his version of Pam's happy sound. Brian would come in and make himself at home on the large bean bag chair near my desk, and every time he did, it warmed my heart.

One of the professional development opportunities I had was learning a system called the "Mandt System," which involved putting crisis cycle concepts into practice, individual-ized tools for de-escalation, and proactive intervention. David Mandt, who developed the program, was the actual instructor for the training, which was excellent and provided a structure for managing aggressive or escalating behavior in ways that prevented injury to clients and staff.

The training was held in the gymnasium in the basement of the Administration Building, quite a long way from the cot-tages, though all campus buildings were connected by under-ground tunnels that made it easier to move students from one building to another if there was inclement weather.

On the first day, just before a brief break was scheduled, I heard a familiar sound coming from the tunnel—shuffling, hands sliding swiftly over one another. I turned to see Brian strolling on in. In a room full of unfamiliar people, he found me. *Now, that,* I thought, *is connection.* That moment confirmed my deep belief that every individual, no matter what their esti-mated potential was, could accomplish things unimagined. At times like these, I wondered about Pam's potential and whether or not anyone tried different things to engage her with her very small world. I was probably the only person in the gymnasium that day who understood what had just taken place.

Another connection I witnessed many times was with a young man who was both blind and deaf. Whenever something in his world was unacceptable to him or he was being led to do something he didn't want to do or he was already in pain and couldn't tell us, he banged his head against the floor or wall, biting his hand, and was becoming very difficult to manage. Chris, our program coordinator, was this boy's lifeline, and it was fascinating to watch her engage with him. If she was called when he exhibited these self-injurious behaviors, he immediately knew she was there, able to calm him down with nothing but a gentle touch. Just like that, the episode ended, and the boy walked quietly around the dorm with Chris.

These new schools of training steered professionals away from a mindset of punishing individuals and instead demonstrated ways to support them through crisis, reinforcing what I always knew: that punishment is not the answer to a child's "problematic" behavior. These programs helped adults protect themselves and the children using the techniques they taught. So often, crises that are often exacerbated through punishment can actually be addressed through conversation and role-play.

Things were going well in my role as a psych tech. Then, I discovered I was pregnant again. I continued working at RSHS until my son was born on September 23, 1982, at which time I returned to running our daycare. This time, we did a major renovation to our garage, which meant we no longer had a garage but now had a functional, bright, and colorful space.

Amid all of these other changes, it took me a long time to realize that my husband's behavior was not going to change, and it was finally time to gather the courage to recognize that things were not going to get better—ever.

For the first time, I saw a therapist. When I found myself explaining what was going on and that I had made up my mind that I wanted to end the marriage, she recommended I read a book called *Getting Them Sober*. I was furious. For the first time since we met, I was no longer interested in rescuing Mark.

But the therapist suggested I read the book first, and then we could talk about it, and I eventually agreed, hoping that, at the very least, it could be a beneficial resource regarding my brother Martin, who had not had the opportunity to receive counseling when his alcohol issues became apparent. As it turned out, the book explained how family roles were established when there is a problem like alcoholism, but I saw the parallel to families dealing with a physical or mental disability. These were the roles described in it:

The Scapegoat, the family member who bears the brunt of blame and resentment. I saw how my father was the one in our family who immediately went into shame if he felt a mistake had been made or if something unsettling happened.

The Hero, who tries to balance out negative emotions in the family. Wayne seemed to be the family member who attempted to draw attention from negativity by always doing the right thing, staying within the lines, and hoping his behavior might change the dynamics. The Hero does these things in an attempt to prevent emotional pain.

The Mascot, who often acts out by cracking jokes or making light of serious situations. Martin had always played this role, using humor to escape the pain of the problems and reduce tension in the family by creating a distraction.

The Enabler, who seeks to protect the person with the "family problem." From my perspective, my mother was the person within the family who attempted to protect the others, especially my father.

The Caretaker, who takes on the caretaker role and often sacrifices their own needs, prioritizing how everyone else is feeling while often neglecting their own feelings and needs. This was my role in the family system.

Despite my initial irritation that the counselor had suggested this book, I ended up grateful for the insights into my complex family dynamic, which had been a source of such frustration over the years. Here was the help I had been waiting for. I clearly recognized the roles we played, though they switched around from time to time.

Feeling the relief of this understanding, I immediately made another appointment with the therapist. This time, I would attend with both of my parents and Martin. I knew I was taking a risk, but I hoped this might give us all the chance we had been waiting for.

My spirits remained high throughout the session, as my family members seemed to be receptive to and understanding of what each other shared and heard from each other and the counselor.

Once we stepped out, my father changed his tone. "I tried to sell a car to that lady's husband," he said. "Anyone dumb enough to be married to that son-of-a-bitch is not someone I am going to get counseling from."

He refused to discuss it any further. That was the end of that; the spell had been broken.

You may write me
   down in history

With your bitter, twisted lies,

You may tread me

in the very dirt

But still, like dust, I'll rise.

~ Maya Angelou

THE UNTHINKABLE
HAPPENS

One evening in 1982, as I was just getting myself and Amber ready to leave my parents' house after having dinner, the phone rang from the bedroom. It was unusual for a call to come in at that time, and I accompanied my father to the bedroom as he went to answer, wondering if something had happened.

"Hello, Mr. Avery?" I heard a voice say on the other line.

"Yes," my father answered expectantly, with an edge that made me listen carefully.

"This is Darroyl Simms. I'm the superintendent at Custer State Hospital. I believe we have met before. I'm sorry to bother you so late."

"That's alright," my father said. "Is everything okay?"

"Well, it's very difficult to know how to go about this, but I have just been informed of something I must share with you about your daughter, Pamela, who is our client here."

"Just a minute. I want to get Deloris on the phone," he said into the receiver before shouting for my mother to pick up from the kitchen.

I stepped closer to my father as he allowed me to listen in.

"Hello, Mrs. Avery," the superintendent continued gravely. "I was just telling your husband I have called to inform you about something that I've just been informed has happened. Unfortunately, an employee here at Custer State Hospital was interviewed today by the Department of Social Services regarding allegations that he had sexually assaulted two of his daughters."

"Okay," my father said with uncertainty. "What are you saying?"

"During the interview, this employee confessed not only to the incidents with his children but also to having sexual contact with our residents here. We have reason to believe that Pamela may have been one of the victims of his sexual abuse along with two other residents here at Custer."

"Oh my God," my father said haltingly. "Are you serious?"

The world around me seemed to blur away as the man on the phone continued to explain that the sheriff's department was still gathering information, assuring my father it was an open investigation that would be treated with the appropriate level of severity and that the sheriff's department would be launching its own investigation as well.

"Is she in the hospital?" I heard my mother's meek voice interject sadly.

"No," Simms responded. "Based on the information we've managed to gather from the interview, we believe the incident took place about two months ago. Grantham is in custody now and unable to cause any further harm. As far as any charges directly related to your daughter, that will likely be up to the state's attorney. I just wanted to make sure you were informed and assure you that we will be cooperating with the sheriff's department to the fullest extent possible."

By the time Simms was remarking on how Grantham was the last person in the world he would have suspected of something like this, we had all fallen silent. It was a face-saving comment on Simms' part, but I wasn't convinced. Perhaps Simms hadn't suspected anything, but how could such behavior go unnoticed by the residents' caretakers? Perhaps if the superintendent had ever actually seen or had a conversation with Grantham or listened to what his co-workers were saying, he would have heard another story. Perhaps they would have told Simms he was the last person they should have hired had it been up to them. Perhaps if families were able to keep in contact with those who actually spent time with the residents, they would have sensed something was going on.

Paired with the treatment I had witnessed firsthand during my recent visit to Custer, I felt a rage I had never before experienced in my life.

"Trust me," Simms wrapped up, "If we hadn't heard from the Department of Social Services and the sheriff's office, we wouldn't have had a clue about this."

"Okay. Thank you for calling," my father said numbly. "Please keep us informed on what is happening." When he hung up the phone, he looked at me and sat heavily on the bed, placing his head in his hands. When he looked back up, his jaw was set tightly in an attempt to gain control and not cry. "Be stoic," I could just about hear him say. When we walked back into the living room, my mother was doing the same.

My mind was racing. None of this made any sense. How could this happen to someone unable to speak, unable to protect herself? Who would do this? And my parents ... they had been through so much already. How could they make it through this, too? Who should they tell? What would they say?

"How do we tell Wayne and Martin about this?" my mother asked, finally breaking down.

There was so much information we still didn't have. My dad stared at the pattern on the bedroom carpet, then got to his feet and paced from the bedroom to the kitchen and back again. His jaw still clenched, he looked to be asking himself what he had possibly done to deserve this.

I couldn't help but bring to mind the various moments over the years when one of us had felt tempted to get Pam out of there. I imagined my parents, too, were reviewing all the significant events of Pam's life, as well as the developmental milestones she didn't meet. Instead of keeping track of her first steps and her first words, their memories of significant moments in their daughter's life included a traumatic birth, the inability to crawl or communicate, going to Custer, and, now, a sexual assault at age twenty-two. My parents had made the hardest decision of their lives, thinking it was the best thing for all of us, just for it to result in the unthinkable happening. I suddenly felt so much pity for them.

"I'll call Wayne and let him know as soon as I get Amber home," I offered. "Call me when Martin gets off work, and I'll come back over and help you tell him." I gave them both a hug and went home.

At home that night, I thought repeatedly about that phone call and how the Custer State Hospital superintendent seemed to be waffling a bit when he said no one would have suspected Grantham would do such a thing. I tried to imagine how this had happened. Who was this nurse's aide? How long had he worked there? How could he have done such a thing? Where could it have even been possible, and when? Was Pam awake and alert? Did she recognize this man? Had he taken care of her for a long time? Was this the first time anything like this had happened to her, or had she been violated before? Was she in pain? Scared? Did she wonder why no one was helping her? Was she wishing her family would come and take her home?

When I thought about what happened to her, I could think about it and describe it based on just that—thinking. Feeling it was something different altogether, something harder to find and put into words. In families who share a painful or burden-some secret—a problem that they feel alone in—communica-tion is indeed impacted.

It is one thing to describe statistics about how people with cognitive disabilities are more susceptible to sexual assault, to explain that sexual violence against disabled people is a silent epidemic, often overlooked both within and outside of reproductive health, rights, and justice circles. According to the Bureau of Justice Statistics' 2009–2014 National Crime Victimization Survey, people with disabilities were more than three times more likely than nondisabled people to experience serious violent crimes such as rape and sexual assault. In addi-tion, having multiple disabilities can increase a person's risk of rape and sexual assault, and children with mental health or intel-lectual disabilities are almost five times more likely than their nondisabled peers to experience sexual abuse.

It is another thing entirely to dive deep into my own feelings. When I allowed myself to feel, it seemed like I might lose con-trol. And so this is the part of my sister's story that is hardest to write, the point at which I arrive over and over again, only to pack it back up and set it on the shelf for "a better time." But there is no "better time" for something like this.

After that phone call from Custer State Hospital, we all sucked in our emotions in our own ways, trying to intellectualize and make sense of what happened rather than feeling the depths of our pain. When we told Wayne and Martin, they, too, were full of questions none of us could answer. Visiting Custer came up, but my mother quickly decided we couldn't do any more for her there than we could by staying put at home as we awaited more information. After some uncomfortable silence, all we could do was wait and keep each other updated.

And yet I soon started to get the feeling that I wasn't being updated. As the official investigation into what happened to Pam was beginning, I was twenty-four years old, seven months pregnant, mother to a daughter who was not yet four, and going through a separation. Because of my personal life, my parents probably didn't keep me totally informed, not wanting to worry me and knowing I was often the first one to rock the boat of injustice, unafraid to draw attention to our family in ways they wished to avoid.

I wanted to be there for Pam, to put my arms around her like I did when we were little, to tell her I was there and it would be all right. I wanted to assure her that our parents would look for answers and that justice would be served. Even as I was unsure that would be the case, I needed to believe it would be so.

In the days that followed, we continued to wait. My father talked to law enforcement and the state's attorney, but no one really had anything to say. In his impatience, he seemed about ready to take action and go to Custer, but my mother was a very practical person, reminding us that it would cost a lot of money and wouldn't change what had already happened. Anyway, she reasoned, it would be better to wait and go when the staff there knew more. We always looked to my mother when it seemed big things were happening, trusting her opinion and following her lead.

For so long, I had believed in the importance of family support during challenging times, and I believe that if there were anyone my mother would have confided in at times like this, it would have been her sisters. But, in this case, that was difficult, because so many of them worked at the Redfield State Hospital and School. She didn't know what they would think, and, more importantly, neither did my father, who had the final say. Would they be critical of Custer State Hospital's response to what had happened? Or would they somehow defend it? Custer and Redfield reported to the same state review boards and were both state institutions.

As we endured this difficult time, my thoughts occasionally drifted to certain things I had heard about male RSHS employees and some of the young women there. Though I hadn't witnessed or seen any firsthand evidence, people seemed to be aware of certain tendencies to use residents' vulnerabilities to take advantage of them. Some of the young women were flattered and willingly discussed how special they felt because of the attention. One woman I worked with referred to the man taking advantage of her as her "boyfriend," saying he was going to marry her.

I thought about these women's lessened ability to resist assault and about Pam's relative inability to do so. My grandma used to say, "It's a mighty poor specimen of a woman who can't protect what she could cover with one hand." She died before this happened to Pam, and I wondered if she would have modified her proclamation upon learning of this news. My sister may have been a twenty-two-year-old woman when she was raped, but she had cerebral palsy. She was nonverbal, unable to walk, and had significant cognitive disabilities. She was so vulnerable. She had no voice. It saddened me to think that someone would make an awful statement like that and truly believe it. Unfortunately, much of the widespread language around women being assaulted was woefully ill-informed.

Meanwhile, Walter Grantham's story was unfolding on the west side of the state. His connection to individuals at the state hospital came to light during an interview at the Custer County sheriff's office, which was shared with my parents as part of the legal proceedings. Grantham was urged to be truthful and honest as he was questioned concerning alleged incidents of incest with one of his daughters, the interviewer pointing out that being honest with the sheriff, who was present, would open up a lot more options for Grantham. If he refused to be honest, he was warned, it could prove to be a messy situation involving the South Dakota State Penitentiary. Eventually, Grantham admitted to engaging in sexual activities with one of his daughters but denied doing so with the other. The admission was enough to rattle the resolve of parents whose children had been under Grantham's care at a place they had been assured they could trust.

At one point, the Custer County nurse who was present during the interview asked Grantham how he felt about working at the state hospital, to which he replied that it kind of bothered him when he had to bathe the residents and change their clothes. When asked why that was, he detailed episodes of sexual misconduct against my sister and two other residents. The next day, Grantham was interviewed by a special agent of the State Division of Criminal Investigation, and he repeated the same information. It was our worst fear come true, receiving certain confirmation of what had been done to Pam.

As terrible as it was to receive this information, we were relieved the investigation was bringing this man's criminal behavior to light. We were informed that the person representing Grantham requested that the judge handling the case suppress the interviews, a motion that was thankfully denied. In the end, the state charged Walter Grantham with five counts of rape. In a plea bargain, he pled guilty to one count of aggravated assault and was sentenced to ten years in the state penitentiary, where I believe he died.

As this was all unfolding, letters from Custer State Hospital staff came pouring in to reveal details about Walter Grantham's questionable work habits, lack of skills, and poor hygiene. One woman shared that the staff used to go to the coffee room in the morning and that Grantham was not usually among the group. Sometimes, someone would say something like, "Where is Walter, anyway? Why does he always take so long?" But they would brush his absence off, assuming he was attending to a sudden issue or someone in need. Knowing what we know now and that the halls were not monitored during the staff-wide coffee break, it becomes clear how it was possible for Grantham to rape residents at his place of work without anyone else seeing.

Another letter that arrived was from a nurse's aide who was willing to help us but needed to be careful so she wouldn't lose her job. Her own daughter had been sexually molested at the age of three, and when she needed help desperately, no one was willing to get involved.

This aide had been part of Grantham's training when he first started working at the hospital. She had asked if he had ever been an aide before or worked in a place like that, and he admitted he hadn't—in fact, he hadn't worked at all for quite a long time. It had been hard for him to get a job, he explained, and he was really surprised when he was hired at Custer State Hospital. Once he was hired, the aides complained about working with him because he was so slow. One of the aides even reported that he had seen Grantham "messing around" with one of the female residents, though this never seemed to be followed up on.

The writer of the letter explained that she had never before worked in a place where leadership was so uninvolved. Once, she saw a man she had never seen before walking through the corridor, wearing a suit and holding a handkerchief to his mouth. When she asked another aide who the man was, she was told it was the hospital administrator. He never makes an appearance on the floor, the coworker explained, because it makes him sick—hence the handkerchief. The head nurses, too, rarely appeared on the floor to make rounds or check rooms. Perhaps if those in charge had been paying more attention, the unthinkable could have been prevented.

Finally, the letter urged my parents not to get discouraged, explaining that what they were doing at Custer State Hospital really needed to be brought out in the open. Many employees had long questioned and complained about some of the hospital practices, such as a couple who arrived with a little girl about three years old, whom they left locked in the car as they went off to eat lunch together. This happened more than once, and sometimes the girl was kept in the car for even longer periods of time. Eventually, they reported what they saw to the head nurses, who reminded employees to mind their own business. The employees then called the Custer police department, after which they didn't see the couple—until about a week later when the man was hired as a nurse's aide.

As more information was revealed, my parents made the most difficult decision they had made since sending Pam to Custer. They brought a civil suit against the superintendent and the director of human resources for negligence and for failing to follow policy in their employment of Walter Grantham. They didn't know if it would do any good or if it might simply stir things up again, but they had to try, even if it meant drawing some attention to our family.

Their attorneys interviewed numerous Custer State Hospital staff members, who were reluctant to share any information initially but eventually opened up about Grantham. They shared that they heard people at Custer were angry about the case, thinking it might bring about its permanent closure. It must have given my parents some comfort to know that there were people at Custer who supported them, but, otherwise, their decision to pursue legal action was one they would ultimately regret for the rest of their lives.

My parents were represented by a law firm located in Rapid City, South Dakota, who needed to prove that the hiring of Walter Grantham was due to negligence on the part of the human resources manager and also that my sister had suffered irreparable damage due Grantham's assault. The lawsuit was built on the fact that Grantham should never have been hired for a position as a nurse's aide in the first place. He had been living on the Custer State Hospital grounds for several days before he was hired, was quite dirty, and had to be "counseled" by the head nurse to clean himself up. It was reported that when not living on hospital grounds, he lived in a house without running water, so his bathing habits were inconsistent.

Grantham had been unable to complete his application, and failure to complete it was supposed to prevent hiring of the individual in question. Nonetheless, he was hired. Once he was, he was slow at getting his work done and was reprimanded on several occasions. One person testified that he didn't understand written instructions and had to have them repeated in detail verbally. Staff was aware that his children had been taken away from him, and it was reported he was a "peeping Tom." Both of these reports were well known, yet nothing was done.

As an employee of Custer State Hospital, he was required to complete training within the first ninety days of employment, after which point he would be evaluated: first, at the three month mark and, again, at five months. Only then is a new hire meant to go off probation to become a permanent employee.

According to personnel records, Walter Grantham was taken off probation at the end of six months without any evaluation completed to assess what kind of employee he was. Had one been conducted, perhaps it would have been discovered that he was too bothered to perform one of his key duties—bathing the residents.

I have tried to find additional information—transcripts of the trial testimony or documents stating what exactly my parents and their lawyer had been unable to prove. All I know is that there was allegedly no evidence of irreparable damage done to Pam as a result of the sexual assault and that this was supposedly due to her cognitive disability.

Once the case had gone public, letters arrived telling my parents that Pam had been relocated—advanced—to a classroom following the assault. The point being made was that she had actually experienced an improvement in ability. It was their way of saying she was not hurt, physically or emotionally. Astoundingly, they were indicating that being raped had not had any negative impact on Pam.

The local physician who examined Pam per Custer State Hospital's request drew a similar conclusion, noting that Pam was not pregnant, had no communicable diseases, and showed "no evidence of physical trauma."

The physician hired by my parents' attorney, on the other hand, completed a similar evaluation and reported her hymen showed signs of being torn in several places, consistent with a woman who had intercourse, supported by the fact that she was inactive—largely immobile—and had never used tampons.

Pam was raped, but legal language diminished her attack to "sexual assault." This idiosyncrasy doesn't change the facts. There were implications that this rape was less tragic because its victim couldn't fully understand what was happening.

We were issued odd pieces of comfort, like, "Thank God she wouldn't remember this," or "At least she didn't understand what was happening to her." Certain individuals even testified in court that the event had no impact on Pam whatsoever, emphasizing the progress she was continuing to make even after the incident as if no harm had been done—as if my parents were unreasonable for seeking punishment against those who had been responsible for my sister's safety and failed miserably to do so.

The prosecution brought an expert witness, Ellen Ryerson, to the stage. She had worked intensively with individuals who have been sexually assaulted, including those who have been termed profoundly or severely retarded, such as Pam. She testified that an attack such as what happened to Pam has just as severe an impact upon her as it would on any other woman in society. There is no ethical reason why Pam should have been viewed as less of a victim of the rape she experienced, and yet Custer State Hospital seemed to be arguing as such.

The staff at Custer State Hospital continued to dispute various claims being made about its leadership and policy adherence. The education staff also disputed the testimony of Alan Bergman, an expert witness who was not employed by Custer State Hospital and had done some testing with Pamela. His tests showed that Pam was withdrawn in what he described as a fear response. The staff also disputed his attention span testing, saying they didn't believe Pam could maintain an attention span of two minutes and therefore couldn't possibly comprehend, let alone remember, the assaults. They alleged there were no lasting effects of the rape. Finally, both of the defendants denied any supervisory responsibilities for Grantham, placing the responsibility on the director of nursing. The lack of accountability taken by people responsible for the health care and well-being of our population's most vulnerable demographic was disheartening and infuriating.

No one knew how best to help my sister at this point. Mom and Dad worked painstakingly to bring Walter Grantham to justice; without their pushing it, I don't believe he would have spent any time in jail. They also pursued a civil lawsuit to advocate for the state to do a better job at screening people when hiring. They lost, and with that loss came a real sense of failure and renewed shame for my parents.

The aftermath of the trial did not bring the feeling of relief we all badly yearned for. A series of placating comments from others were somehow meant to comfort my parents. Remarks like "At least you can take comfort in the fact that he was not a violent man" only seemed to minimize the rape and Grantham's violent actions. It only left me wondering how anyone could believe that a man who molested his own daughter before raping my sister and several others wasn't a violent person? Rape *is* violence. So is the rape of a young woman who completely relies on others for her basic human care.

Dad continued to question whether or not he did the right thing by bringing the assault to trial. Many people approached my parents after the verdict had gone against them to say they were sorry it had turned out that way, reassuring them they did the right thing. That said a lot, and I agreed with them.

Everyone has their own reasons for telling a story. Three other young women on Pam's floor were victims just as much as

Pam was, but their families didn't wish to tell their stories. Other voices can attempt to tell Pamela's story, but no one will ever know exactly what happened to her on the day she was raped—or on any of the other days, as we later learned.

Even though it wasn't the outcome we desired, I believe the trial had an impact on the screening and hiring practices of state institutions. These changes helped hold people responsible for doing their due diligence and upholding higher ethical standards. It would not change what happened to Pamela, but maybe it resulted in improvements that would help other vulnerable individuals.

We will never know how she felt as she was raped by someone she was supposed to be able to trust. For most of my life, I have strived to give voice to the voiceless, to tell their stories to those who might be able to help. This became my guiding light. Eventually, while working with young girls who had been placed in the juvenile corrections center, I would similarly encourage them to use their voices—to talk to their peers and their parents—and to share whether they thought they were making progress.

However, even as I was focused on giving voice to others, in my own life and marriage, there were times I felt I did not have a voice, or at least that it wasn't being heard.

You're allowed to leave someone you love if they're treating you poorly

You're allowed to put yourself first if you're settling

And you're allowed to walk away when you've tried over and over again

But nothing has changed.

- Rania Naim

LIFE'S TRANSITIONS

The lawsuit against Custer State Hospital wasn't the only hard decision being made in my family at the time. With my marriage, too, recent events had been the final straw.

After being married eight years, I had my second child, Travis, just one month after my dear friend Tracy gave birth to Sigourney. We both had our hands full with our newborn children, and one day she invited me to join her on a trip to Prairie Market in Aberdeen to get groceries. It would be our first outing without babies or siblings and would provide forty miles' worth of sacred space to talk all the way there and back.

I told Mark my mom was willing to watch the kids, but he said he could do it and promised to contact my mom if he had any trouble. By this time, he worked with my parents in their shop, and I could rest assured that he was comfortable reaching out to them if needed. I thanked him and gratefully embarked on the journey with Tracy.

Among other things, Tracy also needed to find a dress for her younger sister's upcoming music contest. We found the perfect one and completed our shopping, making our usual stop at Burger King for a chocolate chip cookie and a large iced tea before heading home to Redfield. Neither of us had really ventured out at all since Sig and Travis were born, and it was a great evening we were both very thankful for.

When Tracy pulled up in my driveway, we were surprised to see Amber at the screen door with tears dried on her cheeks. I removed my things from Tracy's car and told her she should go home before rushing over to pull Amber on my lap.

"Daddy's really mad," she told me in her little voice. "He's mad at you, and he's mad at Travis."

Daddy, I learned, had also gone to bed, leaving Amber scared and teary-eyed as she watched for me out the front door. As I listened to her, my heart fell to my feet. Trusting Mark would take care of the kids and call Mom if he needed help had been a big mistake. Having come home to this, I immediately regretted leaving with my friend that night.

I comforted Amber as best I could and tucked her in bed, checking to see that Travis was okay and then sitting in their room until I was sure both were asleep. Once they were, I walked into our bedroom and turned on the light.

"Shut the fucking light off," Mark growled without moving.

I told him I needed to understand why he was angry and what had happened. This only escalated his anger.

"How many guys did you fuck before you got home from Aberdeen?" he demanded without even turning to face me.

I shook my head in disbelief, knowing that trying to talk to him at that point would only make things worse. So I went into the living room and thought about what I was going to do. Seeing the impact on my daughter and how she had been alone with him in his rage, it suddenly occurred to me that if I continued to stay with him, she would take one of two paths. Either she would believe his lies about me, or she would forever wonder why I stayed and let him treat me that way. With this realization, I knew that leaving him was inevitable. I needed time to think this through and make this very difficult decision, confident it was the best decision I could make for my children.

The next morning, as I was dozing in the rocking chair, Mark came up and talked to me as if the prior night's incident had never happened. As he kissed me on the cheek before walking to the door, I asked how he could think that made up for what he had done the night before.

Turning to me, he said, "You shouldn't have pissed me off."

In January of 1984, I filed for divorce. Thankfully, it was an amicable process, and we shared the same attorney, though he made all kinds of promises again and begged me not to take his kids away. *Begged.* He was convinced I was going to make unreasonable demands on him for child support, limit his visitation, and make his life more miserable. That was never my intention, and I was filled with guilt and remorse. I felt as if I was ruining his life, and I tried to reassure him that he would always be their dad and could visit them whenever he wanted to. In reality, he never shared responsibility for our children, yet he was viewed by many as the "good guy" whose wife was never satisfied.

The damage of Mark's words, from the very beginning of our relationship and every day that followed during our nine-year marriage, lasted long after our divorce. Being characterized by my husband as someone I was not, as doing things I never would have done as a bad person, lives on in my soul to this day. Coming home from work a few minutes late, being asked where I've been, followed by hours of accusations of things I didn't do as I desperately tried to defend myself in vain, my words often twisted to the point that I didn't even know what my truth was .... Episodes like these left me doubting myself on every level. After all, gaslighting was his superpower. If this is what he thought, then I must be doing or saying something that did give others this horrible impression of me.

Unfortunately, closure was difficult for me, as my parents continued to employ Mark even after all that had happened. They reasoned that he would need a job in order to provide child support, but I never fully understood the decision. A benefit for the family, though, was that the arrangement made it easy for him and the kids to see each other regularly as they grew up.

In some ways, Mark's words still lingered in my mind even after we separated, but, in other ways, I was free. I re-enrolled at Northern State College (later to become Northern State University in 1989) and double majored in elementary education and special education. It was a challenge, carrying a full course load while parenting two little ones on my own, but I was strongly driven by my goal of becoming a special education teacher, the kind of teacher I would have wanted my sister to have.

My experiences working at RSHS helped me build connections to the material I was studying, as did my wonderful teachers, especially Helen Grabowska, who taught Educational Psychology. She believed in me and told me the world was my oyster, which meant so much after what I'd been through.

I graduated magna cum laude in the spring of 1986 and immediately started putting in applications for teaching positions. It wasn't long before I received a phone call that I had been selected to interview for a special education position in Huron, South Dakota, fifty miles south of Redfield. My friend, Cindy, who had also been sending out resumes and cover letters for work opportunities, was standing in the Johnson Fine Arts Center when I answered the call from Huron Public School and calmly replied that I most certainly was available for an interview.

When I hung up, Cindy explained that she couldn't believe my response to the long-awaited phone call. "Aren't you happy?" she said, practically jumping up and down. "You have an interview!"

"For me, this is what happy looks like," I replied sardonically, characteristic of the Avery resistance to feeling—let alone publicly displaying—joy.

The interview process was different from what I expected. I had a brief interview with the superintendent and then also with both the principal at the elementary school and the special education director. It was a unique position in the Helen Buchanan Program, named after South Dakota's first female physical therapist, who started a program for students with disabilities on her own before the public school integrated it into a new area of the building.

It was an ideal setup in many respects, with two classrooms—one for early childhood and language development and the other for students with physical disabilities. These two classrooms, a small speech therapy room, a kitchen area, and a large therapy room for physical and occupational therapy made up the Helen Buchanan Program layout. The position seemed like a perfect fit for me, and I was very happy when I was offered the job of working with the students with physical and multiple disabilities.

Before my official hire, there was one more person I needed to give me the seal of approval—Helen Buchanan herself. The special education director drove me to Helen's house, telling me along the way about the history of this incredible woman, who had spent many years working with children I would now be serving.

It was an honor to meet her and talk about a subject we were both so passionate about. In an unforgettable moment, I realized that Helen herself had actually been the one to evaluate Pamela Sue and fit her with leg braces so many years ago when my parents first took her to Sioux Falls to be evaluated for assistance with walking. After our conversation, she must have given the special education director the nod of approval, and soon I was given a contract for my first teaching position.

As I met my students, a small group with various disabilities, I was more and more excited to get started. There was nothing about my professional training that equipped me to work with these students, but my time at RSHS had prepared me well in knowing where to start and what kinds of things needed to be addressed.

Getting the job meant my family had to relocate, which was quite an adventure. Right across the street from Buchanan Elementary was a small daycare center where Amber and Travis, now seven and four, could go. So we moved into a nearby house, and my children adjusted well. The people I worked with were amazing, supportive, creative, and great mentors. I was so grateful to them and how safe they made me feel, and they were grateful for the knowledge I brought with me.

We had so much fun with our students, who were full of life and personality. One day, for a fun and sensory activity, they dipped their feet and hands in tempera paint and made prints on a sheet we spread in the hallway. One student who was in the other classroom could hardly wait to get this activity started. Named Amber, just like my daughter, she was blind, so her sensory experience would be different from others. She was going to be the first one to make her footprints, and she made sure that was what happened. I was looking away and talking to the paraprofessional about which students would be next, and when I turned around, little footprints were already stamped across the sheet. She was delightful.

Being a single mother, I would never have been able to succeed at this job without my parents, who were supportive and helpful, even if I disagreed with some of their ideas. There were times when I woke up in the morning and one of the kids was sick. With a phone call to my mother, she would drive the fifty miles to Huron to take care of them. After all the hard work I had put into getting my degree, I think both of my parents came to agree that stepping out in faith had worked out after all.

During that first year, I was observed by the building principal, the special education director, and a representative from the Department of Education as part of a mentoring program that existed at that time. Winging my lesson plans was completely out of the question, as I always had to be prepared for observation. When my children were well, one of the perks of my job was picking them up from the daycare center across the street and bringing them back to my classroom, where they could stay with me while I did lesson planning and set up activities for the next day, though they, too, grew weary as I worked until nearly dinnertime on some days.

One evening, I was close to tears, sitting with my children in my classroom until late in the evening when the custodian, Pete, came in.

"Isn't it about time for you to go home for the day, Ms. Avery?" he asked me, sensing my stress. Leaning forward on his broom, he lowered his voice. "You know, word on the street is that you are doing a damned good job around here. So keep your chin up, and don't worry so much."

His words were the best evaluation I could have received, and I took my tired and hungry children home to rest for the night.

I was not seeking employment elsewhere, but word about

my hard work must have spread, as I was offered a job back in Redfield. I loved the program in Huron, but I felt it would be easier to take care of my children being a little closer to my parents—and my best friend, Tracy. As I talked to her husband, Pat, on the phone, I asked what he thought I should do.

"Hell, I'll subsidize your move," he said. "It'll save that much in long-distance phone calls."

When I accepted the job, I learned that I would be an elementary resource room teacher. I worked closely with the teacher in the classroom next to me with students who had more significant behaviors, while those in my classroom primarily had ADHD and learning disabilities. We combined our classrooms to work on projects together and brought our students together to bake cookies.

Over time, it became a business of sorts, and we called it Mrs. Z's Cookies because my co-teacher's last name was Zaloudek. One student in my classroom who loved to draw designed a logo for us, and we made a list of our goals for the experience. We wanted our students to learn how to greet customers, take their orders for cookies, and put their purchases in bags decorated with our logo. We also wanted them to work on counting the number of cookies requested as well as the money, separating the coins at the end of our sales.

Mrs. Z's Cookies were magical. Two mornings a week, students went to the Home Economics Room, washed their hands, and took out the frozen cookies from a restaurant supply source. Then, they got out the cookie sheets, looked up how hot the oven needed to be, spaced the dough out across the sheet, and baked them. We started printing order forms that we would distribute to classrooms early in the week, and on Fridays, we set up our wares in the hallway leading to the cafeteria. We made signs telling our flavors of the week, and I listened with so much pride as these students, who weren't necessarily proficient in social skills, greeted customers politely, taking and filling their orders. Our cookie business was a success. This is what happens when students—all students—are engaged.

My colleague and I had some pushback from a few of the other teachers, who felt like these students couldn't academically afford to be spending time in the Home Ec room baking cookies. That was unfortunate, but we knew that the students were working on so many skills that we didn't worry too much about them. The feedback was an example, though, of how our culture doesn't realize the value in certain experiences as much as it does sitting and looking at a worksheet. Sure, we could have stayed in the classroom and talked about a cookie business, but that would not have given any of our students the autonomy they experienced from this project.

All the concepts we incorporated into the project, we found to be successful. One child with ADHD, who was extremely shy, waited on customers with more enthusiasm than I had seen from her and, frankly, from similar businesses downtown. It was inspiring to see the students understanding the concepts we worked on at a much different level than they seemed to using other methods. If anyone asked them about their business, the students showed investment and could easily tell them what they were learning.

One morning a week, we welcomed Tony, who joined the business of making cookies. He used a wheelchair, and the other students wanted to push him. It was another step in the right direction. Though, unfortunately, one day, when we were taking him to meet the person transporting him to and from South Dakota Developmental Center Redfield (SDDC-R), the new name for RSHS, I noticed one teacher kept her students from coming out while we passed by. She shook her head and made a comment to me that she didn't think her students needed to be "exposed" to Tony. I was disappointed, thinking we were maybe past this type of thinking. Her comment took me right back to the five-and-dime store on Main Street, where the clerk said students from SDDC-R did not have any business coming into stores downtown. They needed to stay where they belonged.

Aside from those moments, Mrs. Z's Cookies made me a steadfast believer in project-based learning as a way that children with and without disabilities can learn together. It encourages students to take ownership of their learning and has gained momentum as an inquiry-based teaching strategy that teaches students to learn in the real world, more so than teacher-led instruction. Students need to know how to collaborate with others and actively engage to solve real world problems, to be assessed on their ability to apply content when solving problems as well as their understanding of academic content.

Some teachers are not and never will be open to new ideas in education, even as the curriculum updates to reflect modern educational developments. Those who remain stuck in the past often go through the motions, at times sabotaging their own success and that of their students. Unfortunately, the supposed lack of "evidence" of such programs' effectiveness results in a tendency for many great ideas and programs to be discontinued before they even start. There is something to be said about trying a new program and being a part of building evidence, with forethought into what the evidence needs to look like for it to be considered research-based.

Despite my father's earlier preconceptions about teachers' undeservedly high salaries and the one hundred and fifty dollars I received monthly for child support as a single mother living on a teacher's salary, I had to take an additional part-time job at the

Lamont Youth Development Center (LYDC) in the summer. The program, located on the SDDC-R campus, was part of the Department of Corrections, serving students who had been adjudicated as Children in Need of Supervision (CHINS) or delinquent.

I already had a lot on my plate, also working to complete my Master's Degree in Guidance and Counseling, but I needed the gig so I could buy school clothes for the upcoming school year. One afternoon, as I was getting ready to leave for work, my son told me he wanted me to stay home that night. I made all the right points about what we needed money for and why I had to go. I will never forget the comment that came next.

"I would rather go to school wearing a barrel than have you work all the time."

I was certainly no stranger to the trade-offs single mothers have to make all the time for their families. But, fortunately or unfortunately, I had to continue.

The following school year, I became the program director at LYDC, which paid significantly more than teaching had. It wasn't easy for my children, who liked having their mom in their school building, available for them to stop in and visit any time a daily crisis arose. But I put my heart and soul into the program, sometimes there in the morning to help students get up and back in the evening when they got ready for bed. At the time, I felt like it was just what I had to do, but I regret my long hours there because my children didn't get the attention and support they needed.

If anyone had told me that along my career path, I would work for the Department of Corrections, I would have told them that wasn't possible. But I did, and it came to be one of the highlights of my career, interviewing girls who were willing to make a commitment to working the program before they were officially adjudicated. It was rewarding work, and we made significant changes to the program, including to the actual rule book the students had to memorize as part of their orientation.

Key people who worked for the Division of Alcohol and Drug Abuse brought the idea of Improvisational Teen Theater into our correctional facility based on a program being utilized at many high schools across the state. People on our leadership team joined with people from the division to write a grant for approval to bring IMPROV to LYDC. It was exciting and involved making significant changes to allow all of the juveniles in our program to participate. When our grant was approved, we started planning for this once-in-a-lifetime event. Everyone agreed that the experience should follow the guidelines that other high school teams experienced. It meant that together we developed "norms" for the expectations. Among these were those that were considered "non-negotiable."

The young women involved in this experience were able to get in front of people and act out different scenarios, leaving their audience with a question followed by a discussion of potential solutions. This experience was life-changing for many of our students and all of our staff. Our students participated in a competition with other high school groups. It was yet more evidence to me of the effectiveness of project-based learning, resulting in fewer rule violations, arguments, or other misbehaviors. Our hope was that these young people would be able to go back to their high schools and automatically join a team if their high schools participated.

We went on to write and be awarded a grant to develop an independent living program for some of our students who were old enough, had jobs in the community, and did not have adequate support at home. After we created a home on the fourth floor of the administration building, purchasing everything the students needed to live in this "apartment," they were required to pay rent, which was put into a savings account they would be given as they exited the program. This involved establishing a set of expectations to go along with the increased independence and various job responsibilities, and, yet again, the participants were successful.

Unfortunately, we had little time to evaluate the success of this program due to interesting circumstances beyond our control. The South Dakota legislature had approved a new building to house our program, and allocations were in process. We were told by the secretary of corrections that the program would move to the Black Hills, where boys would now be placed at the Youth Forestry Camp and girls would be placed in some similar kind of boot camp. I was disappointed to learn that our program was being moved and disappointed about the direction it was moving in. And then the secretary mentioned where the program would be moving to: the Custer State Hospital building, which would be closing its doors and relocating its residents to various group homes and community centers.

The news stopped me in my tracks. If Custer State Hospital was closing, what would happen to Pam? The place had never seemed like a comfortable home for her, but she had been there for such a long time. If she was moved to a group home, where would it be? Have they informed families yet? Were we the first ones to hear about this plan? Did my parents know about this? I held back tears as I wrapped up the conversation as professionally as I could.

I was beyond proud of the changes I had played a part in making during my time working with the Department of Corrections. The people I worked with and the girls who made incredible progress while I was there made it an unforgettable part of my career. As thankful as I was for the opportunity to learn and grow, I was heartbroken when the program was dismantled, especially as it later sunk in that the girls' boot camp was based on military boot camps, which meant saying goodbye to the prosocial curriculum, the independent living program, and, in all likelihood, the Improvisational Teen Theater. But it was happening, and there was nothing we could do.

Sadly, I later learned that a fourteen-year-old girl who went to the State Training School's boot camp died from heat exhaustion after a forced run. She had been court-ordered to this program, reportedly for petty theft, and if the Lamont Youth Development Center had remained open, she could have been placed there and would likely still be alive. Those of us who had invested our hearts in developing a program like LYDC were saddened to hear about girls being put in four-point restraints for misbehavior. A high percentage of these girls had been sexually abused, and I can think of few things that would do more to trigger a negative response to trauma than four-point restraints.

I was asked to move with the program, but I was not interested in being part of a boot camp program, even with modifications. We had made so many changes to the current program, offered many more opportunities, and treated the students like the learning adolescents they were—not convicted criminals.

As such, it was time to move on to the next opportunity: the assistant professor position at Huron University (HU). This time, my children and I didn't move. Instead, I commuted back and forth between Huron and Redfield. On my first day, I called my mother on my drive back to Redfield.

"You better get ready to teach me how to reupholster furniture," I told her, crying. "Because I can't do this." I was a little overwhelmed, unsure if I could teach at this level, but she reminded me that I had worked hard and knew what I was doing.

I learned how to do this kind of work, and I found she was right. I was quite good at it. Once, during my first year, my supervisor observed me and told me that she was happy I had released my death grip on the podium, which I figured was a positive step. I taught a plethora of classes there, some related to education and some more in the field of psychology. Over the years, I came to love the opportunities to learn from students and assist them in thinking about what they wanted to accomplish.

During this time of changes and upheaval, I met my current husband, Robert—while shopping for a car, of all things. He was working at a car dealership, though he had worked as a chemical dependency counselor, so we had much to talk about regarding the changes we were seeing within the Department of Corrections. The car deal didn't work out, but I received a letter from him. In it, he said it was too bad he couldn't help me find a new car but that sometimes God has other plans.

From that point on, we began corresponding. Friends of mine were skeptical of our significant age difference—I was 42, and he was 55. In spite of others who may have discouraged me from moving forward with the relationship, I was enjoying our time together.

We talked about everything. I learned that he had become a chemical dependency counselor after going to treatment himself—more than once. This was perhaps the only thing he had in common with my first husband, although it was still years before Mark would go to treatment himself.

I admired that Bob had been willing to do what he needed to in order to have a different kind of life. We dated, talked on the phone for hours, and sent cards and letters. When they met, I especially loved his easy rapport with Pamela and how he tried to help me be more relaxed around her. Not only was he comfortable coming inside the building with me when I visited my sister, he felt comfortable actually spending time with her. Even when I was stuck in my own cycles of pain and anger and misunderstanding and seemed to be surrounded by family members who were locked inside of their own pain, Bob would soothe me. "As long as we love each other," he would say, "We will get through anything." After some time, we started to talk about marriage, and I started to think about what was next for my career path.

Around this time, after I had been at HU for two years, a friend of mine told me about a job at Children's Home Society (CHS), a residential facility where children were placed, often by the Department of Social Services, with the goal of reuniting families. Looking into the position, I saw there was also a Day Program in education that called to me. Always when I was counseling, I had missed teaching. And when I was teaching, I had missed counseling. It took me some time to realize the two were part of each other.

The job was as a family therapist in Sioux Falls. It would mean another family move, and everything seemed to be happening fast. I calmed myself by reasoning that if I was chosen for the position, I would just make my decisions then. I drove to Sioux Falls, had lunch with Bob, and went to my interview.

Within a day or two, I was offered the job and made a bold move to accept it. Leaving Redfield was a big change, and many times, I doubted my decision, especially because, this time, it seemed like it would be for good. My parents and I had often touched on the idea that I would be near them—forever and always. My children tried to celebrate with me, but it was difficult. It was my own experience of what it feels like to abandon someone else, and I struggled daily with that for a long time. For the next nine years, though, I worked at my new job on the

Van Demark Upstairs unit, and, in doing so, I found work that I loved and plenty of wonderful friendships. Most of all, I began to understand that individuals who share a mission can truly change the world.

My two nearly grown children and his four grown children were impacted, for better or for worse, by my decision to relocate us and also to introduce another family member into our household. Bob and I were married in March of 2000, amidst all of our kids. In a day, I became a grandma with bonus grandchildren. In fact, between all of our grown-up children, there are now sixteen grandchildren and soon-to-be twelve great-grandchildren. Today, we are still together and still believing in each other. We will soon celebrate our twenty-fifth anniversary. We have been through many difficult times, but we have worked through them together—as I have always believed family should.

The various twists and turns of my career may not seem related to my family's experience with my sister, but, in retrospect, they were. Once the family and I were settled in Sioux Falls, I found that the children at Children's Home Society were typically placed there by the Department of Social Services. The children there typically stayed in the residential program and attended the school there for six to nine months, sometimes longer. Many of them came from less-than-ideal living situations, and they all had one thing in common: family problems that needed to be addressed. Hearts that needed to be healed.

I loved working at Children's Home. After a while, when the assistant principal left, I moved over to the CHS school and worked with students who were placed by school districts in the CHS Day Program. In both positions, I got to meet amazing staff and students and learned more and more about resilience—how some people can go through horrific experiences and still bounce back to form relationships, much like I had done in my own life.

Together with a colleague of mine who was the education director at the Black Hills campus, I presented to a number of regional groups of teachers and administrators during this time, speaking about discipline and its role in supporting youth. Our message was quite simple: Build a relationship with the children with whom you are working, whether in a public school setting, a treatment center, or any other type of "system" designed to help children manage behavior. In any case, it is all about relationships. Start out each day with these children as a brand new day instead of making remarks like, "Well, I hope you are ready to behave better today than you did yesterday because I am not putting up with it." It was an honor to model to others what I believed was a more humane setting for children to grow up in.

When I stepped back and looked at my work with these children, I could trace my path back to that little girl in the fifth grade making a commitment to helping people. What I learned in one program traveled with me to the next opportunity, as did my personal mission to change the world. Every single time, that proved to be the case.

Throughout my career, I was presented with little moments to give to others what I had wished so much for my family. While working at SDDC-R, I often overheard coworkers remarking on how a child's parents just dumped them here, never giving them another thought. I knew firsthand that this wasn't true, and I put my heart into saying so whenever the opportunity presented itself. No one knew what families went through when they made what was likely the most difficult decision of their lives.

And so it was with compassion that I regarded the children as well as their families. When preparing for family visits, I always went the extra mile to be sure that they were ready, nice and clean and in their best clothes. After finding Pam, sitting all alone on that Saturday afternoon, unhappy and unclear, I knew how important the moment of reunion was for all involved. I knew that each time family came to visit, whether for a meeting or an appointment with the family therapist, seeing their loved one clean and nicely dressed, eliminated one concern for them. It said that their child was cared for, loved, and with people they could trust.

The love I held for my sister, Pamela Sue, I wanted to pass along as I communicated to the families in this way. Pam had paved the way for all of my opportunities to help others. There is no telling what direction my life would have taken had I not had her as my sister.

A nd He will raise you up on eagles' wings

Bear you on the breath of dawn

Make you to shine like the sun

And hold you in the palm of His hand

- Michael Joncas

ANOTHER LOSS

Pamela was going through her own series of changes, too. She had been transferred to South Dakota Developmental Center Redfield when Custer State Hospital was closing, just as I had been forewarned it would, and, in 2002, she was moving again—from one of the Cottages at SDDC-R to a group home in Huron.

On moving day, I met my parents and Pamela at the group home. It was warm and welcoming and a much quieter environment than the Cottages had been. One of the first people I noticed there was a young woman I had worked with when she was very young at the Helen Buchanan Program in Huron. Seeing the comfortable environment and a friendly face eased my mind, and my parents and I felt this would be a good change for Pam. To make her room more homey, we bought a nice dresser for her, and once we felt assured that she was settled in and well taken care of, we said our goodbyes and headed back to our respective homes.

Then, on the last day of the year, my father called to tell me that Pam was in the Huron hospital.

"The nurse at the group home called," he told me in a shaky voice. "She said Pam is very sick, that it might be pneumonia. We're going to Huron right away."

After years of working in patient care, I wasn't surprised by the diagnosis. Many individuals who are reliant on being fed by others often aspirate liquids or solids into their lungs, which then can result in pneumonia. I knew how serious this could be for weakened individuals, and I immediately called my daughter, Amber, who was living in Redfield at the time. She agreed to meet us all in Huron, and I got ready and left.

When I arrived at Huron Hospital, my parents and Wayne were already there. As soon as we all stepped foot in Pam's room, we knew she wouldn't remain with us for long. Her breathing was slowing down, becoming more shallow. My parents both had tears in their eyes as they watched her intently. Wayne wanted to take the sadness away, and so did I, but we didn't know how. Sometimes, the greatest losses are silent.

Pam had been at her final home only a short time when she died from pneumonia at the age of forty-two. As a family, we began the task of planning her funeral in Redfield. My dad wondered whether there would be many who remembered or even knew about Pam. At her service, though, there were many extended family members, along with plenty of others who had cared for Pam over the years. Some of them accompanied us home after the ceremony to provide company and help us eat some of the wonderful food that had been kindly brought over by friends and neighbors.

Sitting together at my family home, I listened as others shared stories about Pam, occasionally sharing my own. At one point, I took note of my dad, who seemed so uncomfortable that I feared he might unravel. He stood up and left the room. This time, I followed him.

I entered the library behind him, where his back was turned to me. He bent over, crying like I had never heard him cry before. I walked closer and placed my hand on his shoulder. For the first time ever, with a little encouragement, he didn't suck it all back in or try to brush it off. I felt how overwhelmed he was—by the deep loss we had all experienced together, by the caring people who had taken care of Pam and how they really seemed to *know* her, and by the spirit within Pam that had always longed to be known.

Through his tears, my father spoke to me. He said that the decision to take her to Custer, followed by the decision to file a civil suit after the rape, had been taking up all of his space. I encouraged him to come to the kitchen table and listen to the stories being told in the other room. He looked up at me, and it was like he had finally realized that people had really cared for Pamela Sue.

As we went back to the other room together, my father no longer bothered to hide his tears, nor did I. As grateful as I was for all of the love Pamela Sue had inspired in others, I was saddened to think about the life my family may have had, had we talked about Pamela Sue with these people before. Had we gone to visit her more often and gotten to know her better instead of only doing so when we thought it was most necessary, like on Christmas Eve. Our visits to see her had always been constrained by the limits of the pain we were willing to feel rather than based on the love we all wanted to share together.

Throughout my life, the fact that Pam wasn't in our home has always simmered on the back burner. I don't know that I will ever really get through the grieving process of losing her for good. Somehow, during this heartbreaking time, I went back to Miss Marta Small, my fourth-grade teacher, who helped me by finding me and realizing I had been hiding. She was only in Redfield for one year, but when she found me, I found myself, too.

Whether she knew my circumstances, I have no idea, but she recognized my talent for writing and gave me encouragement and recognition for writing plays as a creative outlet. When I learned that she would not be returning for the next school year, the act of writing helped me grapple with the loss of her.

And so perhaps here, too, I am grappling with loss through writing. This may not be my old *Harriet the Spy* journal from fourth grade, but it is the result of many composition books I carried around with me, jotting down my feelings about situations that seemed out of my control. Through the writing of this book, I have had the ability to sort things out and let go of some of what has weighed on my heart. The process of writing has been cathartic for me and brought me to a place of letting go, and it's a practice I have also encouraged in my daughter, Amber.

Amber always had a beautiful ability to speak to Pamela Sue like someone who really knew her, and I am grateful for this. Following our loss, I asked my daughter, Amber, if she had anything she wanted to add to Pam's story. Her response is as follows:

My Aunt Pam,

I don't remember exactly the day I realized your existence, but I vaguely remember watching old home movies you were in and saying, "I HAVE AN AUNT?" I was so pissed that no one had ever told me about you. I was young—I would guess six or seven—but I remember being so angry with my mom. I couldn't understand why no one had told me about you and why I had never met you.

Conversations around you or about you were always somber. Sometimes, they brought tears, even when Grandma and Grandpa did their best to hide them. It wasn't until I was older and starting to study special education that I interviewed them about having you, a child with a disability, and wrote a paper based on that interview.

When asked about the time you were moved to Custer, Grandpa cried for one of the first times I had ever seen about the decision to do so. They explained that there were several reasons—your size and your seizures growing more severe or intense or frequent. I think it was at this time that Grandpa told me about an older brother with disabilities. The ridicule he experienced as a child, he didn't want his children to have to experience, too. They felt it was the only option they had—for the sake of the other children.

While you were living at home, Grandma had you walking with a walker and leg braces, eating with a spoon, and winning local "cutest baby" contests. But the first time they went to see you in Custer, you were lying in a bed, no longer walking or feeding yourself. From the pictures I saw only recently, you looked so ill, with dark circles under your eyes, and so skinny. I hate to think of what really truly happened to you during that time. I know the family took vacations to the Hills to visit you, but aside from that, I don't know much. I don't know if I was really ever told the part about the rape until I was much older.

I remember, when Custer State Hospital closed, you were transferred to Redfield. As a college student—studying special education, of course— who was commuting, I needed a job. SDDC offered me a part-time position with benefits, and I often got to work at your dorm. Every time I did, I would stop by to say hi, explain that I was your niece Amber, and sit with you for a few minutes if I could. Your arms were often spastic, in a bent position, with your hand near your chest or chin. Some of the other workers like to call them your wings. I always thought that was endearing, though I wonder if it annoyed you.

I remember you were petite like Grandma, and you had her thick, dark hair. You always bobbed your head, maybe as a subconscious way to soothe

155

yourself. When you were happy, you had the best smile and would squeal with glee. I remember times when a staff member made a joke and you would laugh along with us from across the room. I also remember your headstrong spirit—when it was time to feed you, it was always explained that you were stubborn, that if you were done eating, you would clench your jaw shut so you could no longer be fed and needed to take supplements. I discovered that it wasn't that you were done eating but that you just didn't like people shoving things in your mouth without telling you what it was first.

Often, I would tell you things going on with our family, and you seemed to listen, sometimes smiling and bobbing your head. One night, I told you that Grandma had had surgery, and you stopped bobbing your head and turned to look directly at me. I was surprised and quickly explained that everything had gone okay and that she was fine, at which point you went back to bobbing your head. Because of these experiences with you, I knew you were in there, in that mind in a capacity we didn't know about. You were physically disabled but not mentally, except that the years of being institutionalized had caused a lot to diminish or disappear.

Then came a change in the way America thought about institutionalizing individuals, and they started moving people to nursing homes and smaller group home settings. A few months later, though, we were notified that you were very sick and not likely to make it many more days. Grandma, Grandpa, Mom, and I were all there, taking turns spending time with you.

One day, around lunch, Mom and I decided to give Grandma and Grandpa some time alone. We had barely left by the time they called to tell us you had passed. It was like you had been waiting for the chance to be alone with your parents again.

A few days after your death, I had my first vivid experience with a vision. I was lying in bed, thinking about your life, and I saw a tiger's eye, which zoomed out and became an owl's eye, which zoomed out further to be an owl sitting on a branch, and then a bright white flash of light. It was the brightest white I had ever seen, and the most peaceful calm I had ever felt came over my entire body and soul.

Because of you, my life's passion has been working with individuals with disabilities, being an advocate and a voice for them. You taught me how to understand each person and the knowledge they are capable of learning and knowing.

Love, Amber.

L isten to the mustn'ts, child
Listen to the don'ts.

*Listen to the shouldn'ts, the impossibles,
the won'ts.*

*Listen to the never haves, then listen
close to me ...*

*Anything can happen, child. Anything
can be.*

~ Shel Silverstein

REACHING
FOR INCLUSION

Ever since that incident on the playground in fifth grade when my friend Elizabeth was called a retard made me a champion for the kids in the only special education class at our school, I remember feeling I would do something good for people with disabilities. Ever since, I have given my professional best to special education and trying to make things better for all the children I served.

Inclusion is important. As educators and parents, it is important to recognize and accept that the least restrictive environment (LRE) refers to the setting where a child with a disability can receive an appropriate education designed to meet his or her educational needs alongside peers without disabilities to the maximum extent appropriate. That is why it is key to emphasize to children with disabilities that they are a part of the decision-making team.

This does not mean that a student has to be able to master all that the others in the classroom can. It does mean, however, that when there are opportunities for a student with a disability to be a part of the classroom, the team can look for ways for them to participate and succeed.

Typically, lessons are designed for the "average" student, which allows average students to learn but means that above-average students are done with their lesson and on to working independently on something else early. Their needs are really not being met. In the same way, the needs of students with more significant learning problems are also not necessarily met. This is where it becomes more difficult.

When I was in elementary school in the mid-'60s, there was an A class, a B class, and a C class—letter grades that served as a creative naming system for the smart kids' class, the average kids' class, and the remedial class, for those unlikely to grasp or master all of the skills. Each class also had its own understanding of what "mastery" of learning meant. This practice of categorizing learners into separate classes eventually abated, and students were combined into shared classrooms regardless of their ability—except for those with disabilities. They continued to be kept separate.

If we teach to all learners, everyone can succeed. General and special education teachers can work together to create a universal design that helps students of all abilities. To do so, the group needs to be together in the same classroom, using the same curriculum, with certain students provided special assistance, such as closed captioning and ASL interpreting assistance from the deaf education teacher when needed, but otherwise experiencing the same overall classroom expectations. Accommodations and modifications should certainly be made to address their challenges, but the students do not need to receive separate instruction entirely.

One of the most revolutionary moves forward for children with significant cognitive delays is Augmentative and Alternative Communication (AAC). There are many ways to use this, starting with very basic pictures and minimal words all the way to carrying a book with layers of communication levels that students can use for conversations and storytelling. Imagine being able to use something for support that allows you to have access to communication with your peers, your teacher, and your family—for example, a tablet app or a communication device to engage with others and be successful in getting your ideas across. Resources like this allow peers to interact with each other in an inclusive environment that provides learning and meaningful social skills to those who have different communicative needs and abilities.

These modern technologies are powerful tools for those who need them for communication. Having been introduced to AAC at Buchanan in the late eighties, they are a gift I've never taken for granted. One of the students I worked with in the Helen Buchanan Program was evaluated for using what was one of the best communication systems available—the All-Talk, which was ahead of its time in providing the ability to program it using real speech by a same-age peer. It was very large and cumbersome compared to systems and devices used today, though, so one of our first challenges was how to make it functional for students who used it. Like my sister, these students may have had cerebral palsy and cognitive delays that made it even more difficult to handle an unwieldy object. But, also like my sister, we knew their cognitive skills were likely underestimated, so we were very interested in exploring whatever assistive technologies we could.

Everyone on the team was eager to get a particular student, Jackie, access to this communication tool. I had the opportunity to meet June Downing, PhD, a national special education leader and advocate for inclusive education. Working with June gave me more insight into how Pam might have been able to communicate had she been offered AAC. Many times, I wished my sister was right there in my classroom so that I could have the opportunity to provide these experiences for her. I soaked up every minute of time with Dr. Downing over the few days she was there and learned so much about how much communication can take place without verbalizing.

One of the very first successful attempts at communication was using an AAC "switch," a large round circle that acts as a power button when pressed. The switch was connected to a tape recorder that played familiar songs; when it was pushed, the music began to play. When Jackie pushed the button, the music played, and there was much rejoicing at the table. We knew that Jackie had contributed the music. This sounds like a simple thing, but for those who are unable to make certain things happen, it is significant whenever they initiate an action that demonstrates cause and effect.

The need to be creative when working with these students is a big part of teacher education, and teachers do not find this creativity in a textbook. Thankfully, many programs exist for teachers to share ideas and communicate with each other, which is absolutely essential. Communication with parents is also necessary, as the goals of a provider may be very different from the goals of a parent, and communication can provide a bridge between the two.

For instance, parents are often unaware of how activity plans are developed and all of the intentional thought that goes into them. Inviting parents into the process, even to be present to see the end result, allows them to see the beauty of the activity, which words do not always capture. Experiencing the success of these innovative classroom solutions causes a domino effect of other creative approaches, leading to more benefits for students. When teachers and parents are on the same page in developing goals and working together to reach them, amazing things can and do happen.

In 2009, I published my dissertation for my doctorate in Curriculum and Instruction. *Reintegrating Elementary Students from Alternative Placements to Public School* came about as an outcome of the experiences I had while working at Children's Home Society with trying to assist students in making the transition back to public school after dismissal from the alternative program. The most important theme I identified is the importance of building relationships with students. One part of doing so during reintegration to public school is by identifying one person for a student to check in with—someone who is open to this student, interested in their success, and able to ask them questions and provide encouragement.

As such, it is necessary for effective communication between specialized alternative programs and public schools to be in place, building a bridge between these two environments. But, all too often, there are barriers to the construction of that bridge. Timing is a big problem: Even though progress reports are sent to the public school to provide some information on when reintegration will take place, scheduling misalignments often lead to a communication breakdown. When adequate communication tactics are in place, students who leave alternative placements often experience success in their new environment. For many of these students, whose behavior often resulted in missing out on opportunities to demonstrate leadership, it is their first time experiencing such success.

Transitions that take place between elementary and middle school, or middle and high school, can be especially difficult for parents to imagine—even more so when children have had the same supportive paraprofessional for a year or more. Transition meetings, ideally attended by the former and future teachers and paraprofessionals, are extremely helpful—but there is often little time in the program schedule to support laying the groundwork for success in this way.

Even with sufficient preparation, there are challenges for all students making big transitions, though they can be eased with adequate planning. A solid plan for success includes devoting enough time for each student's meeting, however long that is, and carefully documenting what the meeting covers to prepare for staff turnover. Parents' concerns must be addressed, and they often involve the same types of questions. Will my child need a one-on-one paraprofessional with them throughout the day? How will my child know where to go? If he or she is late to class, will it be counted as tardy? Everyone at these Individual Education Program (IEP) transition meetings should be prepared to answer the parents' questions so that the students and families feel more comfortable and taken care of.

The team can provide support by arranging for a paraprofessional to escort a child to class and ensure they have their supplies for the next class, to gradually encourage the student to be more and more independent with time. Maybe this staff person walks them all of the way to class at the beginning of the year before gradually tapering the route so the child learns to complete it on their own, reporting this progress to parents as it happens. Everyone wants students to be able to move independently from class to class with their supplies, and initial measures of support can help them get there.

Transitions do not always involve moving from one facility or school to another. For preschool students, one of the biggest concerns is when a student is non-compliant when asked to sit in a circle. Sometimes, the student meanders around the room, looking for something to engage in. In this case, the student is not successful at making the transition to circle time, even as he or she may be otherwise engaged in what is happening, following along, singing the songs, and performing the actions being asked of the student.

Now, I know that compliance is expected, and likely for good reason—even in preschool. But many things that get reported about students, such as someone needing to sit some distance away from the others, for whatever reason, seem a little unnecessary to me. Is it really necessary to make a problem out of this behavior?

Working toward compliance, what if instead of directing the child's attention to where they should be sitting, they are just encouraged to join the circle whenever they are ready? We can create activities that invite students to join in while still letting them have some choice in the matter. In most cases, when the student sees something interesting, they do move closer to get a good look, even without being redirected or having everyone wait for that student to take their seat in the designated area. We can respect students' need for space while continuing to invite them in, and, typically, this method is successful.

Once, I was in an IEP meeting with a seventeen-year-old male student who had been placed out of the district in a specialized day program. This young man had a cognitive disability and extreme behaviors, which included throwing objects, tearing up the classroom environment, removing clothes, urinating on the floor, spitting, and being physically aggressive. For years, these behaviors had made it difficult for him to function within a classroom without considerable support.

On the day of the meeting, he quietly sat next to his mother playing a game on her cell phone. We were well into the process of determining his eligibility to continue to receive special education services when, all of a sudden, the cell phone rang. He made a noise and immediately threw the cell phone forcefully across the table. Without taking aim at anyone, he barely missed the social worker's head. Next came his shoes. Staff tried to calm him down, but he lashed out at everyone.

More staff was called in, and they moved in calmly until they were standing on each side of the boy, squeezing inward with their bodies. They said very little, gave him calm squeezes, and reassured him he was all right. He slowly began to calm. His mother, in tears, told him goodbye and left to get back to work. This momentarily made him re-escalate, but the staff continued to stay close. His teacher gently ran her fingers through his hair. In one of the signs that his "behavior" was over, he began to cry and apologize. He was remorseful. The staff held his shoes out to the side and asked if he was ready to put them on. He raised a foot and then the other, putting each shoe on as the staff began to move a small distance away. Then, one of them asked if he was ready to return to his classroom. He stood, they offered him his teenage mutant ninja turtle backpack, and he put it on independently before walking out.-

This intervention was successful, the duration of the behavior was minimal, and it was managed by two people and another close by. I had seen other times when five or six adults were not able to contain him, and injuries were sustained. Progress was possible.

Throughout the years, I've heard people describe students as fine until they are expected to do something—calm and well-behaved as long as no demands are placed on them. Maybe, just maybe, what's wrong here is our expectations.

What if we went into the students' world, instead of coercing them to come into ours? What if we worked on what we noticed day after day to come from a place of positive rein-forcement? How can we become more observant and take more time to find out what really does reinforce positive behaviors for each student? As adults, we can study our students and learn from what they have to teach us.

When I had the opportunity to observe elementary students with a variety of significant needs and behaviors, I learned a lot. One time, when the students had completed an activity and were instructed to return to their seats, one boy didn't comply, even after multiple requests. Simultaneously, a parent was bringing her child into the classroom and explained they had come from a doctor's appointment. The student who hadn't sat down walked up to the classmate, stroked her arm, and looked at her with genuine concern. Once again, he was directed to sit down, and, once again, he did not sit down. Instead, he walked to get a tissue and brought it to this child's mother—and, indeed, her child needed a tissue.

What could be wrong with this picture? This student was very watchful and concerned about his classmate, and yet the focus had been on his unwillingness to sit down, which was viewed as non-compliance. There was no reinforcement for being a good friend, showing empathy, or helping a classmate. Sometimes, the most amazing things happen when we are observing something else with different expectations. This may sound like an affront to good behavioral programs, and anyone who has been educated on these knows it is important to be consistent, but there are times to step back and see what we are missing. By doing so, we learn about what kinds of things we may build into a child's day when they are not compliant with directions.

After retiring from the Sioux Falls School District in 2021, I went to work as the supervisor of the Navigator Program at

South Dakota Parent Connection (SDPC). While there, I had a conversation with a mother whose daughter was in the transition process. No real plan had been discussed for this student even though the parent had requested one, and, one day, the mother received a call from the school asking why her child was absent.

Alarmed, the woman grabbed her keys and got ready to find her daughter, who had been dropped off at the front entrance like she always was and had been seen entering the school building. When her mother arrived at the school, she was greeted by a staff person, reassuring her that all was well and her child had been found. In the locker room. Alone.

Was this child safe? Probably. Had she been afraid when she realized she was alone in the locker room? Probably. I am an avid supporter of building independence in all students, but schools cannot drop the ball in making a transition plan for success.

I think about the students with whom teachers work every day. The students don't fit neatly into our "boxes," so teachers must work together to imagine another box that would fit better. I've long had this unsettling feeling that we are missing the boat, that we are focusing on too many things that don't matter and not enough on those that do.

While educators know that their responsibility is to provide appropriate education, parents are involved with all aspects of their child's life. Parents need the professionals who are involved in their child's well-being to listen to and be invested in their input. Teachers and administrators often move too quickly past this information, citing they are only responsible for the educational side of things and that other matters like doctors' opinions have no place at the table. Parents live with the whole child, though, which gives them a holistic picture of their needs. Teachers have to be open and willing to listen, even when that means adding things to the objectives that might be required to meet the child's needs in areas beyond education.

It is my firm belief that every time a student with disabilities undergoes a transition, the parents endure another period of grief. Families often work with a small team of professionals who have been visiting their home for years, sometimes since shortly after birth. These services look very different in early childhood, and moving on is part of the process. Every experience of one support team coming to an end, though, is a loss of people who have understood and supported them, provided a listening ear, and given feedback on how their children have grown under their care.

As children with disabilities grow and progress, they and their families experience staff turnover, new and often larger environments with more students, and different expectations. With each significant change is another opportunity for a feeling of grief and loss.

Even as teachers enthusiastically prepare for an initial meeting and plan objectives for a new child's transition, for parents, this is not their first rodeo. They are not coming to these initial meetings with a novel perspective or a fresh set of eyes. They may have an issue that has gone unresolved and must be addressed, or they introduce other concerns that change the whole dynamic for the IEP team. My hope is that teachers and other service providers will recognize that this is a normal dynamic and can hear the parents' points of view, recognizing the impact of a transition for their child and the whole family.

For parents, there are always ways to prepare for these meetings. What is the most important thing they need teachers to know about their child? What do they want for their child?

Likewise, for teachers, it is important to clarify what is most important to the parents. What may be a first meeting together with this set of parents, these parents have likely been through many such meetings and might be hanging on to expectations that this one will be different. They may be anticipating different strategies will be offered this time, weary of hearing more of the same. It is important to take time to honor parents' opinions at the one time at the beginning of the year that they get to use their voices.

In my experience, helping students acclimate to a new environment by providing additional support is imperative for a successful transition. As children grow, entering new environments means getting more responsibility. Especially when transitioning from elementary to middle school, students go from one classroom and often one teacher, not having to keep track of their things or classroom locations, to navigating multiple class periods located across a campus. This is all new—for everyone. Why would we expect that students with unique needs wouldn't need additional support at the beginning until they are comfortable navigating more independently?

Schools are working toward inclusive education, but the process has been slow in many school settings. New devices and apps are being developed every day, but we have a ways to go and more to learn. When we pay attention, communicate, and listen to each other, we get closer and closer.

Every time I walk into a classroom, I see my sister in the faces of the children. With adequate training, we can support these students to become independent as they attempt tasks. When they are successful, it gives me chills.

Pamela had no exposure to these ideas, but I can imagine her working with these materials and with the other children in spite of their similar physical challenges. I will always wonder how much richer Pamela's life would have been had she been born a couple of decades later than she was.

'Hope' is the thing with feathers–
That perches in the soul,
And sings the tune without the words
And never stops at all

- Emily Dickinson

FORGIVENESS

In 2016, my mother passed away at the Eastern Star Home in Redfield. Amber lived just across the street from there, and I was able to spend a lot of time with Mom in the last few days of her life.

A young woman who lived there and had been injured in a car accident just days before she was to be married had a communication device she used to talk to people. In spite of her accident, she was constantly smiling and spending time with her parents.

One particular evening, as my mother and I walked past the young woman, my mother looked at me and asked, "Is that our Pammy?"

Surprised, I reminded her who the woman was, and we shared a few tears, remembering that Pam was with us no longer.

I am forever grateful for these few days with my mom, tucking her into bed at night just as she had tucked me in as a child.

"Just a mother and her daughter—that's us," she said before she closed her eyes that night.

As I heard her words, I felt Pam's presence with us. I knew she was there comforting my mother, too.

My father had been by my mother's side since she had moved into the nursing care facility. As saddened as he was to lose her, he was glad to be able to move into the independent living part of the facility; by this point, he already knew all of the staff. It truly felt like he was going home.

He was meant to move there on Monday, but on the Friday night prior, already in his slippers, he said, "I might just as well go there tonight, don't you think?"

"If you are ready to go, I'll see if they're okay with that," I said and asked the director, who agreed.

"Welcome home, Kenny," the staff warmly greeted him that evening.

My father adjusted very well to the Independent Living Program. He liked being able to go out into the dining area and pour himself a cappuccino from the machine, to come and go as he pleased, including for long walks and bicycle rides. Every now and then, I would receive a phone call from a friend from Redfield, who happened to be the mayor at that time.

"I hate to call you about this," the polite but hesitant voice would begin, "but are you aware that your dad rides his bike down the middle of the road?"

I assured the friend I would talk to him about it, knowing that most of the people who lived in Redfield were plenty aware of my dad's commitment to walking and riding his bike.

"I was just in the turning lane," Dad explained when I asked him about it.

I let it slide, not bothering to mention that there were no turning lanes in Redfield at that time. I knew my father had never gotten over having to give up his driver's license, a story he told over and over and often got newly upset by. There was nothing anyone could say to help him accept the loss of independence, and I didn't want to fight to take away another piece of it.

As I was walking down his hallway during one of my visits, a nameplate on an apartment door not far from his made me stop immediately. It was the name of the physician who had delivered Pamela all those years ago—the one my father despised and had always blamed for Pam's disability. I talked to the head nurse there and explained that if they were moving residents around to see where they fit in best, it would be best if they could avoid putting my father and this individual at the same table. I gave a brief explanation about them not being in the same circle of friends, and they honored this request.

A month or two later, my father mentioned this man in conversation, saying they had sat together at coffee. This news surprised me, and, at first, I wondered if Dad remembered who this man was.

Seeing the surprise on my face, he said, "Sometimes, things happen and there is no one to blame."

Whatever conversation had taken place between him and the doctor who had played a part in Pam's disability, it had been facilitated by an angel. Maybe that angel was Pamela, bestowing on our father the gift of forgiveness.

In some ways, Dad was different with others than he had been at home with us, where we were often bound to a restrictive dynamic. By contrast, he was often open and accepting with others, carrying on a conversation with anyone who would participate. My siblings and I often teased him about his easy ability to give and assume trust with others, even walking into stores and discovering he didn't have his wallet, assuring the clerk he would be back the next day with a check. It always worked.

In my dad's final years, he finally seemed to give himself permission to be joyful. He told and retold stories of us and our neighbors, and his laugh was more authentic than I'd ever heard it, even over silly things. He often talked about conversations with others that meant so much to him. He was a man who knew who he liked, and it seemed that humor was finally the binding characteristic.

What we had felt as his children and grandchildren was that it was all a comparison, a competition, and that we didn't quite measure up. We longed for recognition and validation from him, to know that he was proud of us. As I learned from the staff at Eastern Star and the friends who visited him, he had always been proud of all of us and of who we had become. It was time for me, too, to forgive.

The truth is that most of us are resilient and have the ability to bounce back, even from unthinkable challenges—and we had all gone through our fair share. After his divorce, Wayne moved on but was alone and, I believe, lonely for a very long time. In his devastation, I suspect that the one thing he needed to hear more than anything else was, "If you want to come home, it's okay."

Wayne worked hard, received promotions for his hard work, and was a loving parent who made some mistakes, as all parents do. He remarried, and remains so today, to a wife who is loyal and unfailingly supportive with the tenacity of a lion whenever she feels he is being overlooked or worn down. His wounds of abandonment are deep, and, because of his wife, he is participating in his life rather than passively watching it go by, which is the pattern in my family.

Going home may not always be an option, but sometimes we need to hear it—that our life isn't over, that people love us, that the sky isn't falling. We need to hear that our children will be alright even when we are unprepared for what happens and feel too empty to know how to comfort or explain any of this to them.

In his life, my father had a difficult time accepting divorce, and each of us went through this process. He knew there would be times when his grandchildren would be with us for some holidays and special events but not others. As Wayne's daughter got older, Dad developed an attitude attributing her absence to her not wanting to spend time with us. He was angry about the whole situation, ashamed of divorce and how it affected his relationship with his grandchildren, based on his oddly twisted perception of things.

I was often a buffer of sorts. There were times when I was talking with Robin on a regular basis, accompanying her for walks in her neighborhood and times when there were very few conversations. All these years later, my brother would maintain that he "did the best he could," stressing that it wasn't easy for him. Perhaps it could have been resolved by him putting his arms around her and saying, "I don't remember it quite like that, but I am sorry you felt that way." Forgiveness goes a long way.

All of these responses to difficult situations could be traced to the communication patterns our family developed long ago—not communicating, not confronting, letting things be. I wish we would have learned these lessons before it was too late.

Robin also shared with me how much she loved her grandfather and how it always made her sad when she talked to him because he often became emotional and started to cry. Forgiveness.

The distance remained there for Robin's whole life, which ended too quickly. Sadly, she passed away in April of 2021, on her first day in hospice care, from breast cancer that had metastasized to her liver and bones. My brother and his wife and Robin's mother were all there when she passed, united, and I know Robin felt their presence. I know that she felt loved by both of her parents, and I am sure that forgiveness *finally* took place.

In recent years, I have become even more open to new ways of communication, believing in the power it can hold in a variety of forms. A blessing I have experienced has been assistance from a friend of mine who is a psychic medium. I was first invited to meet her in a friend's backyard for a group reading, and it was beyond anything I had ever experienced before. I didn't know what to expect and observed as she threw questions out to the group for participants to answer as they felt spoken to. She specifically asked us to confirm what we felt was ours, and we all waited and spoke up when we felt that was the case.

At one point, the medium asked if I had a sister who had passed. She also asked questions about my mom and told me they were both there with us. Immediately, I started to cry.

Since then, she has been able to facilitate communication between me and Pam. Pam was eager to assure me that she had forgiven me—that, in fact, there was nothing to forgive. I was a child, as she was when she left. She told me that I'd been too hard on myself and needed to get out of my own way in order to live my life. This resonated with me deeply.

I have had many conversations with this psychic about different things, and I have felt since beginning this book that Pamela has been guiding me every step of the way, filling in the gaps for me.

In recent years, Pam has finally become a more frequent topic of conversation. My brothers and I talk about our time with Pam and what it was like to live in our home after she left. We have moved past our resentments and questions about who was most responsible for Pam being taken to Custer. Clearing away the bitterness leaves us with more opportunities to speak our individual truths and listen to one another and even laugh about some of the characteristics we carry. It turns out we can relate to the Caliban Syndrome in our own ways.

My children, now grown-ups with children of their own, have also recognized some of the traits that were passed on to them by my generation. They reflect how the adults before them often see obstacles as a crisis, treating joy as an unfamiliar feeling.

While taking family photographs at Martin's second wedding, the photographer said, "This would be a little better if you all didn't look like you were facing a firing squad."

The comment prompted the nervous Avery smiles those who know our family will recognize. We have shared some wonderful laughs about that photo session since.

Over the years, I have learned to speak to my adult children about how I was impacted as a child, not having realized how I was passing all of that down to them. Interestingly, both of my children have found their life's work in the fields of education and healthcare, which I've always viewed as going hand-in-hand.

My daughter, working in a private program for students with autism spectrum disorder, recently told me a story that lifted me up. She was assisting in a situation with one child who was non-verbal and was struggling to calm his body when another child interrupted. When redirected, the other child went into the next room over and picked up his friend's communication device, insistent that he had something important to say. He brought it back and asked a question about what he wanted to do. Play trucks? This was represented on his device. The non-verbal boy nodded, calmed down immediately, and was given the opportunity to play trucks, just as he'd wanted. Communication is a key to so many other behaviors.

When COVID hit, the rules and precautions put in place were very difficult for my father to understand. Staff at the Eastern Star did everything they could to keep their residents safe, but there was nothing they could do about restrictions to visits. What was most difficult was separating those in Nursing Care and those in Independent Living. The loss of social connection was tragic.

My father died in 2021, after being moved to the nursing care side of the facility due to complications from COVID. Martin, now a pastor, united us all in prayer over him, where we remained in stillness long after he was gone. As she so often is, I know Pam's spirit was there with us at that time as well.

Now, I hope that we allow our shared stories to give us peace. Peace for placing her in Custer, peace and gratitude for holding us up when we learned about the rape and the trials that followed, peace for the missing pieces Pam's absence left in each of us, and, finally, peace that would be hers after death. Finally free from all of the limitations she experienced, all that remains is love.

There is someone walking behind you

  Turn around, look at me

There is someone watching your footsteps

Turn around, look at me

There is someone who really needs you

It's my heart in my hand

Turn around, look at me

- The Vogues

MY LETTER
TO PAM

Dear Pamela Sue,

Every year when fall arrives, I think about your birthday and all of the birthday celebrations you didn't have. After you passed away, I struggled. I thought about your death and your life and how much of your life I missed. With encouragement from my husband, Bob, I followed the spiritual advice of my friend, Paula, to write a farewell letter to you, pour out my feelings in it, and stop trying to hold everything back as I had been doing for as long as I could remember. I finally finished the letter, and it was a helpful exercise. But it didn't help me stop holding my feelings back. I also didn't take the time I needed to grieve. Instead, I took on even more responsibilities, teaching a class instead of only taking two graduate courses. I put my feelings on hold.

One of the things that has always bothered me most is that from the other side, you will be able to see how inadequate I was as your sister. I know you have forgiven me, and I try to forgive myself. When you were born, I was two years old, so obviously I don't remember much about it, but I've struggled to understand why I don't have many memories of you in our home.

Shortly before you died, Mom and Dad came to stay with me and Bob for a couple of days, and Mom brought several snapshots she had found when sorting through some things. These pictures were all of you and me, and it was so clear that we had a very special relationship. It saddens me that I can barely remember it. In these pictures, you are cuddled up beside me, and we seem pretty cozy and happy. I believe that even then, I saw myself as taking care of you.

Times were very different then. It was a time when professionals—doctors, teachers, pastors, and others—advised families to place their children with disabilities in an institution, where they could be cared for by people with specialized training. Parents did not question what these professionals were sharing. In the early 1960s, families were encouraged to move on and told that it would be best for other children in the family, too. Removing children with disabilities was encouraged for the sake of the other children. I was one of the other children, and I was powerless over the decision for you to go away.

I hope you can forgive us for not taking care of you, for not keeping you at home with us. I am so sorry you had to go away. I am so sorry you weren't taken care of sometimes.

More than anything else, I am so sorry you had to experience being raped. That was an awful time—another instance when everyone felt so helpless but had no idea how to comfort you. I am sure you have seen that clearly through your angels.

You were twenty-two years old, and one of the nurse's aides took advantage of you and you were raped by him. He had also molested two of his own children. I can't imagine how vulnerable you were. Our parents worked hard to make sure that this individual was charged and convicted. Had they not pressed the issue, I doubt he would have gone to prison.

I have spent several years telling your story as best as I know how. I have researched and found many reports and depositions of people at Custer State Hospital who were involved in providing your care at this time. The letters some of them wrote shared that many people believed our parents did the right thing by filing a civil suit and that there were things that needed to change.

During this process, there were many things that were discussed regarding whether or not you even remembered what happened to you, whether you experienced trauma when it happened, and whether this had any impact on you at all. One "expert" shared a viewpoint that you were not capable of memory and, therefore, did not remember it. Others stuck with the story that there really had been no evidence, other than the perpetrator's confession, that a rape had actually taken place. It was interesting to me that throughout most of the depositions of staff, there was supposedly no knowledge of the incident that was alleged to have taken place and no recollection of conversations among them regarding why there was a police investigation or why Walter Grantham was no longer employed. It seemed that no one owned up to having any knowledge of or responsibility for procedures being followed—or existing in the first place.

Regardless of what they say, we know the truth.

You moved to South Dakota Developmental Center Redfield when Custer State Hospital closed. This meant that we had more opportunities to visit you. When your niece, Amber, was old enough, she went to work there and took care of you at times. Amber was able to build a special relationship with you, and we, as a family, are grateful for that. In your final days, she was there by your side, stroking your face and talking softly to you. She led the way for all of us to be able to comfort you and each other, to tell you goodbye and let you go.

Pamela Sue, I thank you for being my sister and showing me how to have compassion for others, especially for people with special needs and their families. I thank you for helping me to be an advocate for paying more attention to siblings and their feelings. I thank you for all that I've learned from you. And for giving me the courage to speak up for families and sometimes help colleagues understand that they don't know what they don't know.

Please forgive me. I know you are being cared for and loved much better now than you ever were during your lifetime.

With love,

Barbara Lynn

Prayer of St. Francis of Assisi

Lord, make me an instrument of your peace:
where there is hatred, let me sow love;
where there is injury, pardon;
where there is doubt, faith;
where there is despair, hope;
where there is darkness, light;
where there is sadness, joy.
O divine Master, grant that I may not so much seek
to be consoled as to console,
to be understood as to understand,
to be loved as to love.
For it is in giving that we receive,
it is in pardoning that we are pardoned,
and it is in dying that we are born to eternal life.

AUTHOR'S NOTE

As a part of this story about my sister, Pamela Sue Avery, I have immersed myself in historical documents regarding the ways that disabled or marginalized groups have been treated and how their rights have been viewed almost as nonexistent. While this information isn't directly related to my sister, it is important that readers understand the history of individuals like her and how they were treated prior to the early 1960s, when their stories became an important part of the Civil Rights Movement of that time.

Long before the Civil Rights Movement in the late 1800s, social reformers such as Dorothea Dix revealed the deplorable living conditions of people who were unable to care for themselves, including people with disabilities, orphans, and others deemed a burden on their families and communities. From that time and into the 1900s, many attempted to determine why there had been growth in the number of mentally retarded individuals, and the increased attention to the subject led to the creation of more institutions.

At that point, many states developed custodial institutions, which provided custodial care but nothing more. These institutions no longer encouraged interaction with communities. To demonstrate just how much they wanted to isolate individuals from communities, they began to build them in rural areas, away from the view of people. This was the beginning of dehumanizing these individuals, and such was the state of things in the 1960s when my sister was born.

Also in the 1960s, there was a general increase in the population of America, which meant there were proportionately more people with disabilities. Some argued that this was due to increasing immigration, but regardless of the cause for the population surge, it led to another increase in the awareness of people with disabilities, opening the door to some much-needed reassessments and reforms of the institutional support that had been available.

Exploring this history was fascinating, and, unfortunately, it was fairly hidden. A story I assume most people don't know about—I hadn't—is that of Camp Jened, also known as Crip Camp. After Woodstock in 1969, a group of teenage campers decided to get involved in the disability rights movement. So these teenagers staffed the camp with other teenagers, all of whom had disabilities. It was an experiment in freedom. A time of social experimentation.

An amazing documentary shows that some of the campers became voices for the movement and involved themselves in organizing protests, including sit-ins, where individuals with disabilities took their wheelchairs to the street and refused to move. Later, Barack and Michelle Obama saw the film and produced another version of Crip Camp in 2020, which was nominated for an Oscar at the Sundance Film Festival.

In 1973, legislation was introduced to stop discrimination

against individuals based on disabilities, but it was delayed due to the need to gather information on what expenses would be incurred, resulting in a weeks-long sit-in on the fourth floor of the Capitol in San Francisco. These new activists kept the pressure up, not taking no for an answer, and eventually the non-discrimination bill was passed. These efforts undoubtedly paved the way for the passing of the Americans with Disabilities Act in 1990.

I am often surprised to learn how little some of our teachers who are new to the profession understand about the beginnings of disability rights. Without grassroots movements made by people who cared, legislation likely would not have changed. It's not that public schools simply decided, "This is the right thing to do." Pressure needed to be placed, and tenacious individuals needed to place it.

The path that my life and career have taken me on has allowed me to experience firsthand the deinstitutionalization movement of the early 1970s and the grassroots movement initiated by parents across the United States who wanted more for their children, including a place for them in public schools. That said, it is important to understand that there are no guarantees about ongoing supports being in place for the future.

It is interesting to note that even in 2024, many public school settings include general education teachers who maintain that students with disabilities do not belong in the general classroom. The battle seems to continue and compromises are made, but we are many steps away from inclusive environments. If you are one of these teachers, you can continue to complain about how these students don't belong, resulting in students with special needs never showing up on your class list. It may feel like a solution of sorts, but it perpetuates the idea that teachers do not have to serve students with whom they are uncomfortable.

Today, our country is divided on many issues, and one of them is the future of public education. Those who wish to see public education go away are trying to find ways for federal funding to be available for "school choice," which would allow private schools to be paid for federally. Eliminating the Department of Education, which includes the oversight of children with disabilities and holds schools responsible and accountable, could have drastic implications for all students. Significant losses within special education may be incurred, along with changes in the Individuals with Disabilities Education Act (IDEA) that could marginalize these students, because other options are too expensive.

Of all the court setbacks that have taken place, many are ones I never could have imagined. The Dobbs decision overturning Roe v. Wade, changes to affirmative action, attacks on the LBGTQ community, and protections that had been put into place to support them were removed. It all leads me to wonder where the rights protecting students with special needs under IDEA are headed. Especially given that, as my book is nearing publication, a senator from South Dakota, Mike Rounds, submitted legislation to eliminate the Department of Education. If passed by both chambers of Congress and signed into law by the president, the bill would abolish the Department of Education 180 days after becoming law.

The proposed Project 2025 provides a roadmap for the next conservative president to downsize the federal government and fundamentally change how it works. It calls for prohibiting the teaching of "critical race theory" and eliminating terms like diversity, equity, and inclusion. Written and funded by the Heritage Foundation, it recommends that the Department of Education be replaced and special education funds be funneled to school districts as block grants with few strings attached, including for savings accounts that parents could use to pay for private education.

While I fully support families who choose private education, I have a major concern: Private schools select the students they want to serve, whereas public schools must serve all of them—regardless of whether they have academic "potential," whether they speak English, or whether their tuition can be paid.

When questions arise about how to fund special education, there are no clear-cut answers. But the one answer that needs to remain is our responsibility to serve all students in the least restrictive environment. I fear that changes will be made that will alienate schools from families.

I encourage parents who have a child or children with disabilities to remain active advocates for their children and ensure they continue to receive the services they need. But this message isn't only for parents—everyone who cares about these children needs to be listening carefully, educating others who need a broader understanding of what's at stake, and speaking truth to power at school board meetings, parent groups, and other educational groups. Everyone who cares about these children needs to be listening *now*, before they wake up to a breaking news announcement that the Individuals with Disability Education Act has been eradicated.

When I reflect on the atrocities endured by individuals with disabilities and their families, I think about the rationale for sending children out of their homes and into institutions. In my view, the reasons included their inability to make progress, their ineducability, and their parents' lack of "expertise" to properly care for them. It was determined that these individuals could not contribute to society as a whole, and so institutionalized care was better for all involved. But what have the repercussions been?

I pray that as a nation, we continue to advocate for the rights of individuals with disabilities as well as their families, incorporating all that we have learned. The work continues.

BIBLIOGRAPHY

Axline, Virginia M. (1964). *Dibs in Search of Self: The Renowned, Deeply Moving Story of an Emotionally Lost Child Who Found His Way Back.* United States: Random House Publishing Group.

Burghardt, Madeline C. (2018) *Broken: Institutions, Families, and the Construction of Intellectual Disability.* McGill-Queen's University Press.

CBS Sunday Morning. (2021) *"Crip Camp" and the disability rights movement.* www.youtube.com. https://www.youtube.com/watch?v=7i_ZJxVhdhU

Doby, Danielle. (2018) *I Am Her Tribe.* Andrews McMeel Publishing.

Featherstone, Helen. (1981) *A Difference in the Family: Living with a Disabled Child.* Penguin Books.

Kaufman, Barry N. (1976). *Son-Rise: The Miracle Continues.* HJ Kramer.

Larson, Kate Clifford. (2015) *Rosemary: The Hidden Kennedy Daughter.* Houghton Mifflin Harcourt.

Safer, Jeanne. (2002) *The Normal One: Life with a Difficult or Damaged Sibling.* THE FREE PRESS, a division of Simon & Schuster.

South Dakota Public Broadcasting. (2023) *Leaving Redfield.* www.youtube.com https://youtu.be/D7D1VclHwng

ACKNOWLEDGMENTS

First of all, I want to thank my husband, Robert Sterud, for his love and support throughout this journey. I am so grateful for the times he encouraged me not to give up and to move forward and for the times he patiently listened when I was falling apart, convinced that I could not write this book.

I have been finding the courage to gather the words for this book for many years. I have friends who have read and responded to my ideas and very early drafts. All have encouraged me to keep going. I thank those of you who have given me the courage to complete it, which has been extremely therapeutic.

I am grateful for my childhood friend, Elizabeth, who walked a similar path beside me and knows what it's like to have siblings with disabilities and experience the loss of them to an institution. I am also grateful for the colleagues and dear friends I grew close to at Huron Public Schools, Redfield Public School, the Lamont Youth Development Center, the South Dakota Developmental Center in Redfield, Children's Home

Society, Sioux Falls Public Schools, and South Dakota Parent Connection. You always listened, guided, and provided wisdom, and I have learned so much from so many of you along the way.

I want to thank my parents for bravely doing what they truly thought was best for all of us in 1965. I thank them for supporting my career, even when they didn't understand my reasons for taking the risks and moving on. And I am thankful for family members who listened to me lay out this book, piece by piece, and never once discouraged this effort.

To both of my brothers, Wayne Avery and Martin Avery; my children, Amber and Travis; all of my bonus children—Michelle, Jaci, Jenelle, and Scott—and all of the sixteen grandchildren and twelve great-grandchildren Bob and I have been blessed with. Family is a gift, and through all of these wonderful people, I have recognized many empty spaces in my life where Pamela Sue should have been.

And in memory of my niece, Robin Avery, who always encouraged my book. She passed away from breast cancer before I was able to finish this project. Rest in peace, Robin.

ABOUT THE AUTHOR

Barbara Avery-Sterud, EdD, has spent her career teaching and advocating for the rights of individuals with disabilities and their families. At the core of her experience is her sister, Pamela Sue, who was born in 1960, long before services existed for individuals with disabilities. She grew up knowing her sibling had been institutionalized at the age of six and witnessed the impact this had on herself and her family members. Her relationship with Pamela Sue and the lack of sustainability of this relationship were foundational in all of her professional opportunities.